Facebook Advertising:

The Complete Guide to Dominating the Largest Social Media Platform

The trademarks are used without consent, and the publication of the trademark is without permission or backing by the trademark owner. All trademarks and brands within this book are for clarification purposes only and are owned by the owners themselves and not affiliated with this document.

Table of Contents

Introduction

Since its creation, Facebook has generated a following of millions of users around the globe. This largest social media platform has dominated pop culture and has its own contextual marketing prototype buster. With billions of pictures and videos, posts, status updates, check-ins and web link shares, it is not a surprise that most businesses are now on Facebook trying to find different and unique ways to reach out and connect with this vibrant community. Whether it is a local or enterprise level brand, "Like us and follow-up on Facebook" has become the common mantra.

So far Facebook has not disappointed anyone; it responds well by offering something to everyone – business owners, individuals, marketers, brands, freelancers etc. One of its greatest creation is "Fan Page", which gave way to business pages and helped several businesses by allowing the customers/users follow their activities through the News Feed. Eventually, Facebook designed several other opportunities to create different types of ads and promotions that anyone – individuals or organizations – can use. There is no doubt that these advertisements are different from other conventional ways of advertising but these Facebook-style ads have an embedded social element that allows the marketers and business owners show their potential to their target audience. Additionally, they also have an engagement element that makes them interactive and allows the users to click, like, and share the business pages and events.

There are various attributes of Facebook advertising that are well-known. Anyone can design their own Facebook ads, Facebook campaigns, set a daily budget, schedule the ads, track the performance of Ad Campaigns, etc. We need to look at the familiar and not-so-familiar features of Facebook and see how these ads and overall the social media platform can help you extend your presence and connect with the world. Facebook has the power to reach thousands of millions of users, and this guide is particularly designed to help each reader reach their audiences in the most effective way.

Chapter 1: Understanding the Power of Social Media

To understand Facebook as a social media platform, we need to clarify what social media is and what social media marketing does.

Gone are the days when people used to buy TV time or a column in a newspaper to broadcast a message. Today, people have their own DVRs and they read news on the web. What used to be broadcasted on air to small groups, now happens in huge forums of millions of people. The Internet has given us the power to outsmart the viral videos and we do not have to hire the biggest ad firms anymore. Everything is at our fingertips today!

That growth in technology didn't lead to our enhanced desire to use social media. Humans have always liked to socially interact with people, but in the past, it was face-to-face and technology to do otherwise was not at our fingertips. Today, we have access to various applications that help us socialize and we can do it virtually. The big wave of change came in with the advancement of Web2.0. Before the invention of Web2.0 websites, the online communication was restricted to creating and sharing content on static web pages, which seemed more like e-brochures. During that time, companies used to design their websites and keep the same content for years. However, the technological drift came in early 21st Century and the change was so tremendous that it was tagged as Web2.0. This version of the web introduced various social media networking sites and mobile technology and allowed websites to be dynamic. Technology has completely changed the way we socialize through online communities and networks.

With Web2.0 today, there are millions of active Facebook users, millions of bloggers, millions of Twitter users, millions of Youtube viewers, and people across the world are more connected than ever before. If you are not utilizing the power of this social media, you are losing an opportunity.

Social Media

Almost everything has changed since the Internet arrived. The way we shop for groceries, communicate with friends and family, travel across the globe, and do our business – everything has evolved drastically and in such a short span of time. If there is one thing that has catapulted this onslaught of technological elevation, it has to be the Internet in general and social media in particular.

If you think that you can succeed with your business product or service based on yesterday's marketing principles, you are in for a rude shock. Nothing, literally nothing, works today the way it used to work ten years ago. The number of clients and their expectations is mind-boggling. The speed and churn of business are astonishing. If in spite of owning a great product or service, a dedicated team, and the passion to serve, you have not been succeeding, then I can almost bet on one thing - you have not been using effective social media presence. Just visualize the number of times you do a web search in a day. Millions of search results are displayed in a fraction of a second. Most people hardly ever scroll to the second page of a search result.

First, you are not alone in your business. There are millions of others selling similar products and services. Competition is intense and even having a small edge over your competitor counts.

Second, if your business is not listed among the top ten results, there is practically no chance of it ever being discovered by people who do not know you. This is where your social media presence can help you; it will make you visible to the world. In the end, it will save you costs, drive relevant traffic with high conversion potential, and help build trust and credibility for your business.

According to Nielsen, e-users spend more time on social media websites than any other type of site. Also, it has been reported that the total time spent on social media websites in the US (across computer systems and mobile devices) increased by 99% in 2012, which translates to roughly 2 billion hours in a year. The benefits of using this robust social media platform have surpassed anything in the past to build a presence and increase revenue by reaching the target audience directly.

Leveraging Social Media effectively allows your business to reap benefits of its inherent features like Virality. This is a feature of social media which is the more powerful version of 'word-of-mouth'. There is a great possibility that users will re-share content posted (by another user or business) to their social network. Many social media sites provide specific functionality to help users re-share content, for example, Facebook's share link, Twitter's retweet button, Pinterest pin or Tumblr's re-blog function.

To help you understand what social media is, it needs to be defined in context with our conventional media. While conventional media such as newspaper, radio, television etc. are static broadcast, one-way platforms, social media allows its users to create and distribute the content. For instance, to get your advertisement added in the movie or serial, you have to spend money and the person who is viewing this also needs to spend money. Moreover, if someone disagrees with something that was shown in the news, you cannot send your feedback – your voice can't be heard. On the other hand, a blog post or a Facebook post can be created and viewed for free. Advertisers, as well as viewers, do not have to pay anything to the publishing platform; it just needs to be interesting so that it gets more viewers. Moreover, it facilitates two-way communication. This is what social media is: a group of websites where content is created and published by users and communication happens both ways. Social media helps improve your visibility, expand your business, and strengthen the relationship with your customers by connecting with them. Social media has various forms, for various purposes – social networks, sites that share media, forums, social bookmarking sites etc.

History of Advertising

This is the way most people define advertising: Advertising is one-way promotional, paid communication on mass media channels. According to American Marketing Association, it is defined as the placement of promotional messages in media space purchased by organizations, individuals, or businesses for the purposes of informing or persuading their target audience about their services and/or products. It has been a key element of a brand's awareness. However, if conceived from an online marketplace in its attributes and capabilities, it requires a new archetype.

With the advent of social media, the act of marketing has undergone a major revolution. The basis of advertising used to be creating persuasive messages and placing them on purchased media space to reach an audience. This was considered to be the most effective means of marketing for many years. But humans are never satisfied and hence, the marketers and advertisers continued to look for something different. The dramatic change that shook the advertising industry in 2009 marked the beginning of advertisements made over the Internet. Since then, there have been several changes in this domain; mass marketing moved into a digital era and now the consumer has a more engaged and involved connection with the sellers. Today, marketing and advertising experts have entered an era where there is minimal influence over what the consumer sees, reads, watches, and hears. They have adopted more controlled marketing strategies to offer the world more interactive and engaging marketing. While the focus of mass media has been on broadcast and print methods, online advertising involves more targeted, direct and brand-building tactics for social media marketing. The digital advertising is more about connections, engagements, and shared control, and less about static content. Today, the customers create and control their media content to attain media democracy. There were flaws in the traditional advertising model:

Flaw #1: The main flaw in the traditional advertising model is its tight coupling with the mass media, such as newspapers, radio, television etc. The focus on mass media is on broadcasting and printing. The world was looking for something much more than what mass media offered. There was a need for a platform that can reach everyone and anyone; something that doesn't depend on the size of the audience. This is fulfilled by a web platform as it comprises of infinite websites – niche and general (for mass reach). Advertising on the web could mean broadcasting using a display ad on sites that have mass reach, example Google, or it can be reaching someone 1:1 through targeted messages.

Flaw #2: Another flaw in the traditional means of advertising is that it is a paid communication. Today the definition of advertising has changed. Even some of the most effective forms of online advertising are unpaid or paid indirectly.

Flaw #3: Another big flaw is advertising has been one-way means of communication since its inception where the messages are delivered by the marketing experts to the target audience with the help of ads. This kind of communications exerts limits on the communication as it happens in a controlled manner. On the other hand, Web2.0 brought with it a perfect storm that enabled two-way communication between brands and users. It added an element of interaction or consumer involvement to the world of advertising. Today advertising is more about connections and conversations.

The ad era is over and we are a part of new digital ad era, but the marketing experts do not need to stop using traditional ways of advertising. According to the researchers, the combination of both forms (traditional and Web2.0) has resulted in an overall increase in marketing touch-points, and both methods have their own unique value. The traditional media can certainly not be replaced by the new digital marketing media; it should add to the success of marketing efforts. But one must evaluate all the possible methods and see what works the best for their organization or brand keeping their customer base in mind. In order to succeed and achieve marketing goals, marketers, and advertisers must draw inference about the customer's

interests and see where their attention is
Accordingly, they should proceed to advertise in a w
allows their customers to respond. If they are losing i
in traditional media and shifting toward social media,
advertisers and marketers should also move their focus to
social media to maintain their brand awareness. This, by no
means, implies that Web2.0 is killing traditional marketing
methods; it has just evolved to match the needs of today's
advertising and marketing.

Social Media Marketing

The baffling channels of social media advertising make it
difficult to understand what they have in common – shared
platform or the means of communication. Although these
social media messages look similar to all the messages on
conventional advertising platforms, the interactive attribute
that is embedded in these messages is what makes them
interesting and attracts reader's attention. Social media
marketing is the method of using these services to attract
customers based on your connection and your rapport. This
type of marketing makes use of the latest online technologies
to achieve marketing goals of the advertisers.

Social media marketing comprises of several operations and
methods to generate publicity through the use of these social
websites. Businesses should be where their clients are. Here
are the facts:

- There are more than 1.5 billion people worldwide who
  use the Internet.
- More than 70% of these are habitual of reading blogs.

- Of those who use the Internet, about 40% write their own blogs.
- More than 60% of them are active on at least one of the social media platforms.
- More than half of Internet users have pictures uploaded on social channels.
- More than 85% of the Internet users watch videos online.
- More than 70% of the Internet users visit the social channels.
- Wikipedia consists of more than 20 million articles.
- There are more than 100 million Youtube videos that are viewed.
- Twitter users post more than 50 million tweets in a year.
- Facebook is used more than 80 million hours each day.
- Facebook adds more than 100 million users in 10 months.
- More than 80% of organizations use the social media platform LinkedIn to find candidates.

You can clearly see the reach and popularity of social media channels; it has brought the biggest reformation to society since the 19th Century. It has changed the way we think, communicate, and connect with others. You cannot avoid this powerful platform if you are trying to market your product or brand as it is inseparable from the society of today. If you are a business owner and trying to make your mark in the marketplace, you must create a social media plan for your brand, evaluate which is the best social media channel for your business, and what are the blogs that can be closely connected to your business/brand. Analyze what is available and decide on two or3 social media websites that can work for your business. Next, evaluate and create blogs that will target your intended audience. You can either write your own blogs or include existing ones in your social media plan. By commenting on other blogs and participating in forums, you can make your presence in the marketplace known where your target audience hangs out. The foremost step in social media marketing is selecting the best platform for your business or brand. Social media is your best advertising solution because:

1. It helps you grow your fan-base and ultimately creates sales.
2. Co-create: It helps you create customer-generated content for your marketing goals, which certainly perform better than any other advertising medium.
3. Customer reach: It aids you in targeting new as well as existing customers.
4. Measurement and Analytics: You can use analytics offered by these platforms to determine how your business is performing.

Before you jump into this digital sphere of marketing, look at some of the aspects to ensure social media marketing is actually right for your business.

You need to determine who and where your target audience is. One of the key reasons social media became so popular so quickly is the reach and extent of the online marketplace today. Most products can be bought and sold online. The Internet has become an ideal marketplace and an ideal platform to market your products and services. If your customers use the web for research or shopping purposes, social media is the right choice for you. However, not every business can be successful on the web, and at the same time, it is not really difficult to make your presence known online. Some people say you need to have a deadly search engine ranking in order to get heard or seen. If you do the research properly and find the right tools to get into action, you are good to go. For instance, you can use the free listing option offered by Google Local Business to list your business details to be visible when anyone searches for your product or similar products online. An important factor is that an online presence helps you attract your customer's attention in "reviews". If you have a handful of positive reviews, you can attract others to visit your site.

You have to keep a constant eye on all your competitors to see what they have been doing. Discover their activities and strategies. If you find them active on the forum or attending certain trade shows, you should also attend them. If you see them following certain communities, pages, commenting regularly in certain groups, writing blogs, then you should do the same. This way you will not just know what they are doing but also what they are not doing, and this should be your lead to leave them behind.

Deciding on a strong social media plan requires a significant amount of time and effort. You need to spend a lot of time to find out what's trending and what would work best for your business scenario. You will have to spend time every day on a number of platforms, read blogs, check videos, follow your competitors, post regularly, make comments, and add to discussions in the forums and communities to make your presence known. If you don't have enough time for all this, social media marketing is probably not the right thing for you. In that case, you must reevaluate your marketing goals to see what you can do with the available resources (time, money, and effort). However, Social Media has the potential to replace any other form of marketing.

- Time – Creating and setting up ads and campaigns on social media platforms are less expensive than the traditional ads, but if you consider time as money, then yes, social media marketing is going to be an expensive show for you. Social media campaigns and ads do not run on their own, they are quite demanding. If you want to reap maximum benefits from a platform, you need to have lots of time, time, and more time. You need time to set up ads, to monitor the progress, to keep an eye on your competitor's activities, to keep your customers engaged, to comment on related blogs, to be active on forums that are related to your brand, to connect with influencers; these are just a few of the things that you need to do.
- Effort – Put in all that it takes to learn the tricks of the trade. Social media is so vast that no one can ever call himself a master of this domain; there is always something new to learn. Read as many blogs as possible. Learn the tricks from communities and forums where people always share their experiences. Learn from books (like this one☺) that teach you about various social media platforms. Attend trade shows and conferences/sessions on social media marketing.

Size of Social Circle

As the attention and interests of people have moved to an online presence and activities, marketers are now able to track their activities and buying decisions. The increase in a digital presence has enhanced the ability of marketers and advertisers to collect consumer data which can be analyzed to monitor the consumers' activities. Big Data has become a buzzword in the industry and refers to the enormous amount of data that is difficult to process using the conventional applications. According to reports generated in 2013, around 90% of the total data in the world was created within last two years and of this data, 80% was content from social media channels, such as Youtube, Instagram, Facebook etc. Generally, Big data includes data related to transactions, messages, emails, and activities of every description.

Not only is this data enormous in terms of information, it also impacts businesses greatly. According to a global survey conducted in 2015 by Forbes, organizations that are leading in data-driven marketing are three times more able to boost their revenues than their straggler counterparts. The increased data extracted from the social channels is advantageous in bridging the gap between the traditional marketing methods and a data-driven approach. The enormous amount of this data presents immense opportunities. However, marketers today are not that fast in taking advantage of these growing opportunities. Although digital research is robust, only 35% of the marketers use social media content and only around 33% monitor the influence of social networking. The buzz created by big data is not being translated into big businesses, but those who took advantage of this social media data are gaining a competitive edge over their competitors.

One thing is certain – social media is not just a trend; it is an opportunity. If you look at the stats, Facebook grew more than 200% from the year 2012 to 2013, while Google Plus grew by around 800%. Although this is good news for everyone, some marketers see this as a challenge. This is mainly because social media strategy is so different from other conventional ways of marketing and integrating it with the current marketing strategies requires a complete shift in mindset; it cannot be simply added as another advertising outlet. Marketing experts need to accept the challenge and find ways to reap maximum benefits from the increased opportunities and untapped capabilities created by this data.

Until the Internet, budgets used to be a critical criterion for deciding how a brand was marketed – more budget, more brand awareness. But today, things have changed. Even with a small budget, businesses, brands, and start-up firms (big and small) can increase the level of awareness in the marketplace by using social media data. It is the potential of media opportunities that make a difference in improving the visibility of a business and the viral spread of a brand to reach the target audience. Social media is not just for those who have the latest technologies; it also helps those who still use the traditional ways of marketing. Integrating social media data with conventional advertising methods can really pay. No one could disagree that e-word-of-mouth is certainly more effective than the traditional marketing for customer acquisition.

Market experts can reap benefits from social media data. Big brands, small firms, organizations, startups, and entrepreneurs must learn the rules of the new game. Everyone must play this social media game by adhering to different marketing rules. There has been a drastic change in the mindset and this requires a strategic framework to be adapted to integrate the new rules into the existing ones to make marketing efforts more effective in order to meet the marketing goals of different organizations. These rules are not just about opening the accounts on all the social media platforms; the rules are about winning on each platform. Researching and deciding on a solid game plan is the key to winning. And for this, we need time, we need resources, we need a PLAN - a well-researched, well-crafted social media plan. Big Data means big opportunities, and if you can learn to utilize the social media data correctly, you can explore and exploit the scale and scope of marketing in today's e-world.

From Controlled to Engaged

With more and more media channels, it is difficult to keep the consumer engaged. The consumer is constantly flitting back and forth between listening to the radio, watching television, texting friends on mobile apps, and browsing the Internet for information. Marketers today really need to adjust their strategies and marketing plan from a controlled one to more interactive, engaging one. The success of a brand has more to do with real-time, global, electronic information that is always available to the user. This shift requires much more effort than just buying consumer touch-points; social media is a very different platform. Marketers are now required to include all sorts of brand messages because the new media requires brand communication by not just marketing partners but also by consumers. It is a less controlled form and more engaged and there is a need for marketing experts to move from an interruption-driven model to an engagement-driven platform. This change needs to happen without losing the customer's attention and interest. Understand one thing – social media is not trying to wrest control from marketers, it is just offering an additional opportunity to maintain control. The integration is the glue that holds the practice of marketing and public relations together in an engaged fashion.

The drift from mass media to interactive, digital media is shifting the focus of control from advertisers to consumers, offering more engaged and directive styles of marketing. To gain the advantage of this new methodology, marketing experts should integrate and manage all brand-related content whether it is consumer generated or organization generated. When marketers open a 2-way communication with the customer, it is a collaborative approach. Companies act as a hub of information and are responsible for maintaining a constant flow of brand information as they respond to customer's needs. Marketing2.0 appreciates the power and capabilities of social channels to develop and spread brand messages, enhance customer relations, and offer marketing insights and products.

Shifting to this new collaborative model is not easy; it is certainly challenging as it requires new tools, strategies, plans, and interaction. This transformational journey will produce several opportunities. Research has proved that the change has led to building direct relationships with customers. The voice of customers generates brand awareness, builds loyalty, and enhances the brand value. And in the world of social media, loyalty is infectious.

Selecting the Best Social Media Platform

No single platform can do justice to your social media marketing activities. According to researchers and studies, users rarely stay active on one social media platform; they are likely to toggle between multiple platforms. They might have their profiles active on one, two, or three platforms, so find the platforms where the majority of your potential customers are active. It is always better to market on multiple channels than to focus on just one platform. This way you can reach different categories of customers in different ways. However, it is almost impossible to market on every platform, all at the same time with the same focus. Money is not the concern, but your efforts on each of the mediums will take up your time and efforts. So, you need to find where most of your customers hang out and invest most of your time there. Start looking at your audience and see where they make most of their buying decisions.

- **Know your audience**: Analyze and learn where your customers are spending most of their time and money and where they are most engaged. Engagement is how much time they are spending on different platforms, what they do there, how they interact with other users, and how they behave. While you are monitoring this, also look for mentions of your competitors, your brand, your industry, and your product to understand the level of activity across the platforms. You will eventually discover that there are two to three social media platforms that match your criteria, and where you can see high levels of engagement of your target audience. This is where most of your customers spend most of their time and money, make their buying decisions, and also connect with other users.
- **Know your industry influence**: When you look at the influence of your industry, you might find a long list of potential customers that you might want to

establish a connection to make them aware of your brand. There are various tools available these days that can do this job for you. Some of these tools are – Marketing Grader, Klout, etc.

- **Assess each social media platform**: Now that you know your customer base and the influence of your industry, analyze various platforms to see what each has to offer you and your business.

Facebook – the market leader in social media marketing – brings with it a very casual and light environment that requires an effective, active social media strategy. With over 1.44 billion monthly users, Facebook is definitely the most widely used form of social media. Ever since it was founded, Facebook has been revolutionizing the art of connecting with people online. This is definitely the best tool to make use of and I highly recommend every business that is new to Internet marketing to kick-off by promoting on this platform. One of my clients who was extremely skeptical about its effectiveness finally gave in and gave it a try. And voila! Marketing via Facebook did the trick.

It's not rocket science to learn how! First, start a page and share it with the people you know. The next step is to ask them to share it with a larger audience. Once the page is all set and people start viewing it, you need to make sure their eyes and minds are glued to the page. For example: Suppose you are going to start a chain of ice cream parlors and you create a page with the name of 'XYZ Ice creams'. You can then post pictures of your parlor, create an interesting layout, and post articles related to your business. Put the virtual world out to the real world!

Facebook allows you to view each and every detail. You can monitor the number of page views you get. The count will help you to decide between two options: either to promote further or to improve the current page. Once you see your fans viewing your page, keep them engaged, ask them questions, and ask for their feedback. Once you receive some good feedbacks, post them on the page so that the others know the worth and quality of your product. Keep posting as much as you can, this helps to increase the chances of more people stumbling onto your page and being attracted to the products you have to offer.

If you are a business owner, you can start by looking at the Business Page. Pay utmost attention to the layout as it is one of the key aspects that gain customer's attention. Facebook is a platform where people come to socialize and chat, so keep the tone friendly and light. Facebook provides various formats to create ads, such as video ads, photo ads, slideshows, carousels, etc.

Create a logo to represent your company and post pictures related to your business on a daily basis. But make sure your page looks professional with all the necessary contents.

Classical Facebook Ads are another way to promote your business. These Ads include a click-through link, an image, and a headline with copy. The link can be to your Facebook Page or another website. These Ads appear in the side-columns and can increase your page viewers by thousands in a matter of hours or days.

Google Plus – a social media platform that has been giving competition to Facebook – entered the market as just another social media platform, but today it serves as a niche platform. On Google Plus, you can share content, upload images and videos, share links and posts and get connected with people. A great feature of Google Plus is Google Circles that help its users to categorize their followers into small groups or circles. This helps users to share specific information with a specific set of people (circle). For instance, if you want to offer a discount to a specific group of allied customers, you can put them all in a circle and share this special discount with them. Don't forget the Hangouts feature of Google Plus that gives you the power to host conferences. For instance, if you are an artist and you create handcrafted bottles. You can set up a "DIY – How to make handcrafted bottles" session on Hangouts. You can call out to your community members and ask them to leave a feedback for you, which can later be fed into social media.

Google+ allows you to take advantage of the Youtube engine, blogger, and other applications they offer. Everything you post on any of these apps appears in your Google+ profile so that the people in your circle and others know what you are doing. You can extend the life of your content by using the option Google+ Embedded Posts to share your Google+ posts on your blog. This prevents your posts from being lost in a stream of other posts that others may share. Asking open-ended questions or just starting up a healthy discussion with the relevant followers is a great way to attract a number of customers and builds a good connection with your followers.

For newbies, posting an open-ended question may not be the best way to promote their business as they still do not have thousands of followers. For this reason, as a beginner, you have to engage in relevant conversations and promote your business in an indirect way through the discussions. Your engagement in those conversations proves that you are interested in the interests of that community and have something to contribute. This will lead people who are a part of the discussion to check out your profile. Whether they begin to love your page or demand your product totally depends on the way you structure your profile.

Pinterest – one of the fastest growing platforms in the world of social media – is an image-centric medium that has something to offer everyone. If your goal is to drive traffic to your website, Pinterest can help you do that. If you want to drive more sales, Pinterest is the solution. Business owners display their listings and create a brand presence with the help of attractive, unique pinboards. Remember- you must enter this platform with a strong social media strategy that helps you make a presence on Pinterest.

Twitter – another lovable social media platform – helps you display what you are doing to the world. With this platform, you can follow the tweeters, tweet back, and retweet something that is related to your industry or brand so that you can gain more followers. You can mix your brand-building updates with tweets about offers, discounts, and special promotions to engage your potential customers on regular basis. If you like something someone said (related to your industry or domain), do not forget to retweet the post. Answer the queries and comments of other users so that they get to know you. Twitter is all about communicating, sharing, resharing, and commenting. Therefore, use this social media marketing platform to interact with your audience as much as possible. You will see what you can build and nurture. Twitter offers its users various kinds of ads – Promoted Tweets, promoted accounts, and promoted trends. The ads created on Twitter are also categorized based on the campaign objective. For instance, for tweet engagement campaigns, you can promote your ads with the aim of having conversations about your brand and you pay for the engagement.

LinkedIn – a professional social media website – is a great place for everyone looking for some professional help and connecting with people in similar domains. LinkedIn offers a great venue to share content and media with people who share similar interests. It is also a platform to search for people to hire. You can post job descriptions and connect with candidates. LinkedIn permits you to give and receive business recommendations on your profile, which make you look more credible and authentic to your business connects or customers.

YouTube – the number one platform for sharing and creating videos – is another very popular and powerful social media marketing tool. Creating video content instead of plain text is always more appealing. If you are planning to create how-to videos to connect with your target audience, you have the opportunity to go viral. As these videos have the ability to receive high ranking in Google search results, focus on creating instructive and visually appealing "how-to" videos.

Now that you have some information about some of the popular social media marketing platforms, you can decide which one can be best for your business. But first, we need to take a closer look more at the most popular social media advertising platforms – Facebook.

Chapter 2:

The Basics of Facebook Advertising

One of the most important parts of social media advertising is Facebook Advertising. With more than 2.2 billion monthly active users (as reported in the 4th quarter of 2017), Facebook has become one of the most popular and powerful social media channels that can be used for targeted online advertising.

Like the real estate business, the most important quality of a property is its location, we can say the same thing about advertising. You cannot watch a video, check out a site, read a blog, or message your buddy on a social networking site without hearing or seeing a message from advertisers. These ads are omnipresent and sometimes even annoying, but try to see it from an advertiser's point of view – they want to be where their audiences are. And this is absolutely fair. If you want to spread a message or make yourself heard, you might also do the same thing. Of course you will, and especially after reading this ebook, you certainly will. After all, the aim of these ads is to incorporate promotional and persuasive messages into the everyday lives of the target audience. And as the Internet is "THE" word today, more and more people are incorporating this new transformation in their lives.

The world of advertising has seen a tectonic shift with the advent of Web2.0 – from the static text-only ads to online, real-time streaming videos and rich media ads.

Advertisement has changed its shape and definition completely. The focus of this new generation advertising industry has been to stay free of cost for the person who is watching or hearing. People now have their own free email accounts; they host their own sites where they can have all types of discussions. Everyone knows about the world-popular search engine websites Google and Yahoo that help people find information about anything. The revenue these sites generate with the help of ads that are displayed alongside the search results is staggering.

Today, social media space is the hottest place where most of the people can be found. On these platforms, they share their stories, pictures, videos; they communicate with their old friends, meet new people, and join various groups to discuss on forums. Alongside all these activities, are the Ads that we all watch, knowingly or unknowingly. This is the power of advertising.

Today, Facebook holds a unique place in the marketplace – it is full of information about its users, and more and more content is being generated every day, every minute. Facebook knows how to help advertisers use this data to derive important information, without intruding into the privacy of the users. You need to understand how Facebook achieves this, how an ad is created and placed, and the various types of ads. I will also highlight some of the unique features that Facebook offers its users so that you can appreciate the power of this advertising medium so you can spread your promotional messages to exact target audience in a subtle manner that doesn't annoy people, which is the main aim of every advertiser.

The Emergence

While some of the social networks such as MySpace continued to grow in 2004-2005, Facebook emerged as one of its main rival that was successful in dominating the social networking industry across the world. Although this platform was quite similar in its features as its predecessors, it added a layer of security to the user data and standardized the overall experience of searching user data. Facebook offered its users a complete gamut of tools to expose useful content to a restricted set of people – people within their network. Another chapter was drafted in the battle of MySpace and Facebook when Facebook started capturing the attention of students, while MySpace had managed to make loyal young followers in several years. From there, it slowly started expanding beyond the educational domain. In May 2007, Facebook created a developer platform so that the developers can create custom applications to take advantage of unique social graphs of its users. It made its customers available to third-party developers that resulted in an explosion of new apps on Facebook. Various sorts of apps, including gaming apps, were created almost immediately. And finally, Facebook overtook its rival and emerged as a dominant player in the social domain.

The Basics

Facebook has been growing at a staggering rate since the time of its inception and it's all because it fits well the requirements of businesses and individuals. While individuals use it to connect with the world, reunite with their old friends and relatives, share images and videos and see what's happening around the world, businesses use it to promote their brand or products and make their websites more social. When you log onto your Facebook account, you see your Home Page where you can read messages on your friends' timelines/wall. You even see who has commented or liked your posts. While you do all this, you will at least see one ad, which is normally placed on the right side of the page. These are the Facebook ads and anyone can create these ads (if you have the budget to do so).

For businesses, the primary tool is a Business Page on Facebook, which is quite similar to a user's profile but includes certain features that help businesses create and publish content to connect with those who might be interested in that content and analyze their behavior.

Facebook has something to offer to every advertiser, big or small. Here are the core elements of a typical ad that appears on Facebook :

- Title – that comprises of a maximum of 25 characters
- An Image – that is optional but it is always great to have one
- The Message – which is the Ad copy comprising of a maximum of 135 characters
- A link – to another website or Facebook itself when someone clicks on it

If you are a Facebook user, you might have seen ads displayed on the right side of your page, comprising of these elements. Additionally, Facebook adds a link that encourages the users to 'Like' the page or advertisement. If an advertiser is promoting a Business Page on Facebook, then "Liking" it will add you as a fan of that Business Page. If not, you will be asked to vote if you like the advertisement posted by the advertiser. This is one of the ways in which Facebook helps its users utilize the power of ads that appear on the platform. It also makes these ads interactive so that when someone clicks on the Like button of an ad, their friends get to know that this user has liked an ad, and this might encourage them to view that ad too.

Users can also engage in a social action on the ads and are known as engagement ads or social ads. These can include social actions, such as "RSVP" or videos for the user to interact by watching the video from the ad directly.

Facebook is a powerful social media platform that has something to offer to both businesses and customers; it entices all the industries. This is the reason businesses, as well as individuals, are adopting and learning how to use it as an advertising platform by creating Pages, Ads, and Campaigns to achieve their marketing goals, such as:

- Launching products and services: Businesses are using this platform to test their products and services and to run campaigns as part of their launch strategy.
- Improving brand awareness: Companies, both big and small, are learning and adopting the massive community of Facebook using its pages and apps.
- Selling products and services: Some businesses are offering their services on Facebook using the applications that can be easily integrated with their Facebook Page.
- Customer service: Businesses find Facebook to be an inexpensive and effective means to enhance their support channels as these resolutions can be seen by not one but various customers.

Advertising Tools for Each Type

As mentioned earlier, Facebook offers several ways for an advertiser to interact with an audience including:

Pages, Events, and Groups: Facebook Events, Pages, Groups, and Places are available for free for any type of business. These tools have the same social attributes, such as News Feed, Likes, Shares, Comments, etc., which all the users use to connect with their family and friends. In simple words, business owners are able to connect with their customers the same way other users connect with their friends.

Ads: Ads can be either purchased on a Cost-per-impression (CPI) or Cost-per-click (CPC) basis on Facebook. These ads are gaining popularity each day as they help advertisers to reach all kinds of audiences at a much cheaper price. With all the information provided by Facebook users, the platform has a wealth of information about its users that can be used to derive important statistics. Cost-per-click is often used by advertisers who track the ad performance closely and do not want to pay until someone clicks the ad and is redirected to the linked page. The advertiser doesn't pay each time the ad is displayed. Also, each click can be tracked to understand if any further action was taken by the user after clicking the ad. Cost-per-impression is used by those advertisers who want to know the visibility of their ad instead of the action performed by the customer. It shows how advertisers originally used to pay for their online ads. Whenever an ad was displayed on the channel, it was to increase the count of "impressions", and an amount was paid as per the rate charged for 1000 impressions. However, the cost is much less as compared to CPC ads because you are not paying for the performance.

Ads Manager: This tool helps the users manage and measure the ads so that the performance of these ads can be checked from time to time.

Unique Features of Facebook Advertising

Facebook's share of referrals on social media has been growing and is unstoppable. If you have a website for your business, you must use Facebook to drive traffic to your content. One of the powerful ways of doing this is through Facebook Ads.

Today, billions of dollars are being spent on Internet advertising, and a major chunk of it is attributable to the online advertising firms that are trying to find better and more efficient ways of serving the online advertisers. With advancement in technology, websites are now able to incorporate videos, images, and various kinds of flash technologies in their ads to make them catchy. Facebook, today, is capable of providing some amazing aspects to its advertisers and the credit goes to all the information it holds about its users. The information about its users is provided in the form of user-profiles, discussion forums, News Feed, groups, and various other places where the user enters information. The best part is Facebook knows how to collect this information to derive important data without breaching the privacy of its users.

Some of these unique features that Facebook offers users are:

Targeting Audience profiles: For most search engine websites such as Google, all you get to know about a viewer is the keywords he types when looking for something using the search engines. Hence, the ads have to be really attractive to catch the attention of the user who is trying to find something using those keywords. With Facebook, it is different. You can know a lot about the person viewing one of the ads. This is because when someone signs up for an account, he completes an extensive form that asks him everything from his personal information to what he is currently doing, his interests, likes, dislikes, his background, marital status and so on. This information is stored in the profile of each user on Facebook, and this can be offered to advertisers to target profiles that match their marketing goals. Here's an example. Suppose you are trying to advertise a business that sells gifts for weddings. Using your systems, you can run search engine ads by targeting phrases such as wedding gifts or wedding chores. But using Facebook, you can tell the platform to show your ad to only the users who are in the age group 24 to 33 with a marital status of ' Engaged'.

Targeting a specific set within an audience is really important so that you can attract their attention. Know what they are interested in, their likes, their hobbies, their educational background, where they live, what they do and so on. This will help you build your ideal customer profile.

Using Ads that are clickable but do not leave the page: When you click an online ad, it redirects you to another website or opens up another page in a new tab to view what the advertiser wants you to see and do after seeing that ad (post action). However, Facebook offers its users a feature that most other sites do not offer – you can be on the original webpage when you click the ad and perform the required action that the advertiser wants you to do. You will never be taken off the page where the ad was originally placed. Facebook includes another element in these ads that are not found in ads shown on other sites. This is a link or a button called click to action. The link or button later transforms into a confirmation message upon action completion and never redirects the user to another page.

Facebook Profiles

A profile on Facebook is a representation of a user; in a way, they are an extension of their real-life personality. Users share their updates only with their connected groups with the help of these profiles. For an advertiser, this is where the game begins. In order to reach and connect with your target audience, you must understand what they do and what they like doing. Always remember, a valuable Facebook user is the one who provides valuable information from time to time and has vast connections. It is important to keep your profile updated and make it look fresh and relevant to your connections.

It is a known fact that users spend a lot of time on Facebook, therefore, one must appreciate the openness and dedication of these users as they are the ones who will help you in attaining your marketing goals.

A typical Facebook profile includes the user's background, interests, likes, dislikes, education, hobbies, work details, etc. It also lists any page and group he is connected to - from a favorite music band to the preferred brand of shoes. Some of the users are quite open with their profiles and Facebook encourages this strongly for the benefit of marketers. It gives an opportunity to the marketers to use this personal data to derive some potential results. All those who do not like the openness of their personal information can change the privacy settings to keep it hidden from the world.

Although Facebook's original intention for creating profiles was social networking for students, it slowly expanded to people of all ages. However, adhering to its original framework of connecting to others, Facebook always stands by certain rules for businesses and brands. One of the distinctions between a normal profile and a business profile is you must set up a Business Page to represent your business/brand. However, the basic elements remain the same.

Does my business need a Page?

The easiest and probably the best way to make your voice on Facebook is to create a Business Page for your brand. A page is like a home for your business that keeps people up-to-date about your operations, upcoming events, and contact details. It also displays content in various forms, such as text, videos, images, etc. These business pages help you connect with your customers and provide you a means to learn more about what they expect from your business.

The easiest way to determine when you need just a profile and when you need a page is to compare and understand the verbs used to interact on Facebook – Friend and Like (or Fan). You always *Friend* someone who you like or want to become friends with, but you cannot friend a movie or a music band; you can always *Like* them. Another thing, although a film star can have a profile and has friends on this profile, the majority of the public can only Like him on this platform. All public figures can have a private profile with real friends added as friends, but they will also have a page to remain connected with their fans. In simple words, if any sort of marketing is required, you need a Facebook Page.

As Facebook Business Page can be seen by anyone who is available online, you can greatly improve your visibility and positioning of your brand. You are also allowing the search engine websites to find you on the web. Here are some of the important components of Facebook that has made it an important tool for businesses:

- **News Feed/Wall**: Your Facebook Wall is actually a wall of fame. It serves as the key component of a Facebook Page so you can upload content in various forms, such as links, photos, videos, notes, etc. All this generates updates and appears as stories on the News Feed of your friends.
- **Like**: When a user clicks on the Like button of your Facebook Business Page, he becomes a fan of your page. By clicking, he is actually trying to express his interest in your business so that he can read stories about your business in his News Feed. When this happens, it is also visible to his friends who are also likely to like your page and become your business fans. Every page on Facebook comprises of a wall for its users to engage with others by publishing content that interests them. This engagement can help you convert your fans into potential customers. The content that appears on your Wall is known as stories

and appear as News Feed to your fans. Your fans react to these stories by liking and/or commenting on them, and that's where the stories appear on their profiles and in News Feed of their friends. When these friends of your fans read these stories in the News Feed, and act on it by liking and/or commenting, or even by visiting your page directly, they also become a fan of your Business Page. This way the connection grows and you turn more and more fans into potential customers.

- **Status**: This is the update field that states "What's on your mind?". Using this tab, you can add your status update or post something that you feel will interest your target audience. This text will then appear in the News Feed of all those who have liked your Business Page (in simple words, your fans).
- **Info**: It is the tab that gives detailed information about your company – the link, its address, etc.
- **Apps**: You can link various apps to your Facebook Page. There are numerous apps that help you run contests, promotions, deals, etc. So, utilize this feature and reap as many benefits as you can.

Your Facebook Marketing Plan

Facebook has provided an ever-growing audience at relatively low or no cost. But that doesn't mean you take it for granted; you need to come up with a future-proof marketing plan keeping in mind who your target audience is and what is it that they are looking for.

Social channels have brought a drastic change in how we used to advertise our business or products. It has also changed the way we use the Internet; rather than using it just as a source of information, we are now using as a means to connect with other people across the globe. Facebook helps you connect with people who share similar interests with you. Conventional marketing mediums could only shout at their audience by telling them what they have. The world has changed. Today, the high tech marketing mediums offer two-way communication rather than the shouting 1-way approach. Today, we have blogs and communities for its users to comment on what the advertisers are showing them in form of text, images, or videos. There are tools that allow people to have real-time conversations with others and even share their real-time location. With these social networking mediums and tools, your business can reap advantages of technology to advertise your products or brand by electronic word-of-mouth. When a Facebook fan of your Business Page comments a Facebook Event you have created or installs your app on his profile, those actions are converted into stories which then appears on his Wall and in his News Feed. In simple words, a persuasive message that you had advertised is transmitted electronically to other users on Facebook expanding your brand awareness – this is called electronic word-of-mouth.

Before you learn how to use Facebook to advertise your business, you should put together an effective and strong Facebook marketing plan – a way to align your actions with your marketing goals. Here is what you need to do to create this plan:

- Create the value propositions
- Know your audience
- Set your marketing goals
- Create an effective content marketing strategy

- Analyze and schedule your activities

These are the steps in detail:

Create the Value Proposition

The first and foremost thing you need to consider while developing a marketing plan is your business value proposition. This is the unique proposition of your organization that defines how your business is different from other similar ones and why someone should choose you over others. You might want to describe a different value proposition for each product depending on your target audience. Your marketing plan should revolve around how you plan to communicate these unique values to your target audience.

To create value proposition:

You need to know how your business is different from your competitors'. Know what your competitors are up to and understand what your unique offerings are that differentiates you from others.

Provide a unique value to your customers. This plays a key role in developing your messages, and this depends on what you are trying to accomplish using this marketing plan.

You need to define your business goals. Most businesses have certain common goals, such as driving more sales or getting more traffic to their website. Sometimes you may have goals that are unique. Define these unique goals and ensure your marketing plan aligns with these goals.

Know your Audience

You must know your audience – their culture, their views, their likes, their dislikes, where they spend their leisure time, and the information they generally look for. The better you understand your audience and the more information you derive from their behavior, the more effectively and efficiently you will be able to gain their attention through your messages.

Know what makes them tick. Using the power of Facebook, you can get some information about your customers. Using its ad targeting capabilities, Facebook has made it cost-effective and simple for you to identify and reach your target audience. With the help of the Facebook Insights tool, you can get information about all those who visited your Facebook Page – their demography, their interests, their psychographic variables, which define qualities related to their values, personality, interests, and attitudes. For instance, you can request your customers to participate in a questionnaire through your website. You can also analyze the comments people have posted on the Facebook Wall of your competitions to see what is it that makes their customers remain loyal.

Know what motivates them. Now that you know your target audience, know what motivates them. Everyone in this world likes to feel special, and your audience is no exception. So, make them feel special by telling them they are important to you and you are always there to hear their concerns. Most importantly, offer discounts and special promotions – everyone loves them!

Know where to find them. One of the key advantages of Facebook advertising is that it gives you access to crucial information about its users that they provide while creating their Facebook profiles. Based on the privacy settings set by the user, you can see their marital status, their educational background, where they stay, where they are from, what they do, what have they done in the past, places visited, their likes, dislikes, hobbies, political views, religious views, employment details and so on. This information is crucial. In the past, business owners used to pay a lot of money to get this sort of information about their customers, and thanks to Facebook, today everything is at your fingertips, and that too is free.

Facebook search is a great tool to identify your ideal target audience. All you need to do is to key in keywords in the search field and it will display all the pages, users, groups, and communities related to the typed keywords. If you are looking to connect to an old pal or want some information about someone who shares similar views as yours, the Facebook search is THE tool for you.

Set Your Marketing Goals

You need to know:

- what made you decide to start marketing your business,
- if you want to make more money,
- if you want to see increased numbers and drive more sales,
- if you want to enhance your brand awareness,
- if you want to generate more traffic to your website.

All these are achievable goals and you can achieve all of them using the power of Facebook.

Create an Effective Marketing Strategy

For any business to thrive, it is important that it makes itself popular with as many people as possible. To achieve this, you need to have an effective marketing strategy – you need to run promotions. Facebook offers several marketing promotional tools for spreading the message to users; it helps your marketing message reach your fans, the friends of those fans, and anyone who is interested in what you are offering. Some of the opportunities presented by Facebook to those who are looking to reach more and more people are the following:

Facebook Ads: You can buy space on Facebook pages to display your ads. These ads are visible to the targeted people based on the criteria defined by you. If their profile matches your criteria, they will be able to see these ads. Generally, a Facebook Ad comprises of text and an image, and some of them are even paired with videos and certain pages relating to social actions.

Sponsored Stories: Facebook ads convert the activities of your friends and fans into promotions. Facebook Sponsored Stories are paid ads that appear on the right side of the Facebook pages. More subtle than the normal Facebook ads, Sponsored Stories have more impact on the targeted audience.

Facebook Deals: Facebook Deals are created based on the check-ins of people on Facebook when they visit your brand or business. You can run these deals across your business locations or stores and create unique deals in different locations based on what business goal you are trying to achieve.

Facebook Marketplace: Facebook Marketplace is a website dedicated to those who want to sell personal products and/or services. Facebook Marketplace is quite similar to the classified ad website that lists real estate, cars, rentals, and anything for sale.

These options offer great business opportunities to brands to improve visibility in the marketplace. The task is to evaluate each of these opportunities and decide which will work the best for your marketing goals. For an example, if your marketing goal is to drive more targeted traffic to your site, you must try Facebook Ads. If you are looking to just selling your products, Facebook Marketplace is the option for you.

Facebook News Feed Work

News Feed is the flagship that appears on your Facebook Homepage. It shows you several stories and updates from your friends. Stories refer to the actions taken by your friends on Facebook. It could mean sharing an image, sharing an update, creating an event and so on. You might also see stories from some of the pages you have been following. But in simple terms, News Feed is an algorithm – an intelligent algorithm that tries to show you things you are likely to be interested in. It learns from you and adjusts itself to show you what you like to see.

Facebook uses an algorithm to automate the selection of content that goes on the News Feed of each user. You need to know how it chooses what to show in the News Feed of the users, and how to have more people see your content. However, it is not easy to understand how the News Feed work as the underlying algorithm is always changing.

Facebook's ultimate goal is to show those stories in the News Feed that are most engaging and interesting. There could be several stories that can appear on your News Feed but Facebook ensures only the relevant content appears and is formatted in slots so that you can easily browse through them. Also, the content is ranked and displayed in order of relevance. For instance – if your sibling moved to another city, this news appears on top and others appear below the important one. It prioritizes the stories that you might like, comment or share with others, and this is referred to as engagement. To make the feeds more engaging, it also asks for users' feedback in the form of a survey or by creating focus groups because the more engaging the content is, the more you would want to come back for more. This will accomplish the goal of connecting and engaging more people and also earn revenues from the ads marketers publish in the News Feed.

As more people join Facebook and each of them creates more pages and share more content, the available space each one gets in the News Feed shrinks due to increased competition. People seem to be spending more time on News Feed and hence more stories are appearing. All this declines the natural reach of your post and content in the feed – reach in terms of the number of people who should be seeing or clicking on your post vs. all those who are eligible to see it. This is clearly the result of more people posting more frequently and the percentage of people who see your content shrinks. To counteract this side-effect of the growing number of people on Facebook, you must know how the News Feed algorithm works.

Facebook knows what to show you in your News Feed. Each story that appears in your News Feed is assigned a personalized relevancy score which varies from person to person. Once the scores are assigned, stories that are most relevant appear at the top of the list. To arrive at this score, the algorithm takes into account several different factors but the major ones that decide the relevancy score and the visibility of a story are: who posted it, when it was posted, the type of content, and the interactions with the post.

- **Who posted it**: If you have engaged with a user in the post, Facebook thinks you will be also interested in interacting with him/her in the future. The engagement could have been in any form – liking, sharing, commenting, clicking, visiting his profile or page, being tagged by him in some of his posts, tagging him, reading his posts and so on. This engagement leads to what you see in your feeds and what you don't see. For instance – you don't see posts from your distant relatives who you haven't had interaction in years. Facebook recognizes if you haven't interacted with them in so many years, you would not be interested in connecting with them now.

- **When it was posted**: The more recently a post has appeared, the more likely you are to see it. The algorithm also checks when you were last available to see your updates, and shows older posts on the top if you haven't checked your feeds since they were posted. If you want to see this happening, see the difference in the feeds by checking your News Feed after every hour or so. Then check after a couple of days, and you will see that Facebook will have some important updates ready for you, even if those were posted a few days ago. Facebook ensures you do not miss anything important.

- **Type of content**: Facebook analyzes what kind of content you normally engage with and shows you more of the same – videos, images, posts, events and so on. Each user likes a different kind of posts, so Facebook ensures you see more of what you like.
- **Interactions with the post**: If a post is seen by lots of people, there is a high probability that Facebook will show it to you too. This is because if a post has become viral, it means it is interesting and engaging, and Facebook wants you also to see what's interesting. If a page or post doesn't attract attention from many people, it means it is boring and people are not interested in it.

All these factors together impact what you see on your News Feed. When you interact with posts in News Feed, the algorithm recognizes you and your likes and updates itself when your behavior changes.

Apart from the above-mentioned important factors, there are several others that determine what you see in your News Feed, although they do not impact the feed the same way such as new products.

Facebook News Feed Algorithm Demystified

How can advertisers optimize their posts so that their News Feed gains reach and visibility?

1. Understand how the News Feed algorithm decides the rank of the content of your Facebook Page. If we look at the dictionary definition of algorithm, it includes

steps or a formula that solves a problem. For example, you want to buy an evening dress for a party. You go to an online store and check their catalog to see the options available. You might have certain specifications in terms of color, style, size, and cost. Consider all these factors and then start making light predictions – how would I look if I wear this color, would this style suit my body, is it worth spending this much amount for this dress etc. Consider all the information and then place an order based on your requirements.

When you are thinking aloud, you are actually processing an algorithm within your mind. That is what all of us do each day for almost every task. Similarly, the algorithm used by Facebook consists of several steps to decide how it should rank your content. These steps are – Inventory (what options does the online store catalog have), Signals (Is the party during the daytime or evening), Predictions (Will this style suit my body) and Score (Placing the order).

Inventory is what the algorithm considers when you first open your News Feed. It looks at different feeds posted by others on your News Feed and what you follow.

Signals are the raw facts or data used by the Facebook algorithm to make an informed decision. The algorithm considers all the given data and determines how you might be interested in something. There is a huge amount of data that it takes into account to rank your content – the time of the post, who posted the content, how much time you have and so on.

Predictions are the conclusions that the algorithm makes with the help of signals. For example – will the color right for you, and so on.

Score is what the Facebook calculates after analyzing the signals and determining the predictions. This score is known as the relevance score and it denotes the number that shows how interested you might be in a story according to the algorithm. However, it is just a calculated number determined by Facebook and might not be actually what you think about a story. This algorithm is run each time you log into your account, and that's how you see what you see.

2. Understand the signals that Facebook takes into account for analyzing your content. The most important factors that determine what you see in your feed is what you like, what you follow, and who you friend on Facebook. These are what determines the way Facebook interprets the signals it considers while placing an order for a News Feed item that resonates with the interests. Some of the signals that impact your ranking on Facebook include Engagement (engagement of a post, average time spent on content), who posted the story (negative feedback from someone, and frequency of posts from a user who posted).

3. Understand the Predictions made by Facebook while ranking the content. Facebook takes into consideration many factors to rank your content, such

as the pages you follow, your friends list, and the signals (mentioned above) to make these predictions that include:

- to click
- to spend time with a story
- to like, comment, and share
- if you'll find it informative
- this is click bait
- this contains nudity

All this results in a score, and a News Feed that is different for different users. Below are some of the tips that can be used to create content that reaches as many users as possible –

- ○ Try to have a clean Facebook Page. This means have a page that is free from negative comments from other users. There will be times when you cannot do anything about these negative feedbacks, but try to stay away from them as much as you can. Also, proofread your content and check your links before you post them on to the page.
- ○ Always try to create content that is likely to receive positive feedback from other users. This positive feedback can be in the form of reactions, likes, comments and so on. Also, see to it that this published content encourages your audience to engage and invest their time. Video content is one of the most powerful and effective means to do this.
- ○ Post something that can be shared and liked by others. When you see your audience comments,

sharing and liking your content, it is an indication that they are liking your posts.

- ○ Always look to build an audience by keeping your objectives in mind. If you build an audience that is not interested in what you do, there is no point in having them at all as they will not engage or like your content.

Common Type of Stories That Appear in News Feeds

News Feeds consist of different types of stories (or posts) from friends or people/pages we follow. Although the anatomy of these stories might not be different from each other, here are some of the types –

- **Status Updates**: These are the short posts that your friends publish about what's going on around them and what they have been doing.
- **Photos and Videos**: When your friends add photos and tag others, Facebook creates a story without information about the photo and who was tagged in it. Similarly, it creates a story when videos are published.
- **Links**: Whenever your friends share links to something they read and liked or something that might interest others, a story is created in the News Feed. If you want to read the information in detail, you can click the link.
- **Timeline posts**: These are stories around casual posts that friends write on each other's timeline.

- **Live videos**: Live videos are streamed live from where the person is located. Once it is broadcasted, it appears like any other normal post in the News Feed.
- **Event and group posts**: whenever someone posts an event or group you are a part of, you will see those comments or messages in your feed. These are just like timeline posts; the only difference is that instead of a friend's name, the group or Event Name appears in the post.

Ads in News Feed

Facebook News Feed is not only about posts and updates, they also show ads to the users. The best thing about these ads is they do not replace any posts that appear in the feed; they are just injected somewhere in between these posts, pushing the ones that appear later in the feed. Just the way Facebook has an algorithm to find the posts that appear in the feed, it has a different algorithm that decides what ads would be shown in the News Feed. Even this algorithm assigns ranking to the ads based on several factors and limits the number of ads a user sees in his feed to ensure the ones you see resonate with your likes and behavior. If it shows irrelevant ads, nobody would be interested and motivated to click on them and Facebook wouldn't earn anything from those ads.

The more data you provide about yourself and the more active you online, the more Facebook will know about you. If Facebook knows you well, it will show you more relevant content and ads. That's why you should complete your profile with as many details as possible, and engage with content you like so that Facebook makes it all more personalized for you. You will see more relevant content and will be informed about events, groups, pages you might be interested in.

Control what you see in your News Feed

Facebook gives you the authority to choose what you want to see and what you do not want to see. It provides you ways to teach your News Feed what you wish to see and what's irrelevant – both implicit and explicit. Some of the implicit ways are derived from how you behave on Facebook. If you have been following someone or liking someone's page, Facebook knows you like it. If you have been reading posts from a particular user, Facebook knows you like his content. If you have been joining travel groups, Facebook knows traveling might be one of your hobbies. That's why it is important that you 'Like' things only when you like them and not just to please someone.

Additionally, Facebook also provides you some of the explicit tools to tell your News Feed what you wish to see and what you don't. Each story that appears in your feed comes with a drop-down arrow that allows you to:

- <u>Hide a post</u> so that you do not get to see it again until you unhide it explicitly. This also prevents similar stories from appearing in your feed.
- <u>Unfollow CNN</u> so that you do not see any more posts from the specific page.
- <u>Save it for later</u> so that you can always view it later. This also tells Facebook that you are interested in similar posts.

- Turn On notifications so that you receive an alert whenever something is posted by this person.
- See First option so you can choose pages or people whose posts should always appear on the top in the News Feed. This is particularly important when you are following a particular person.

Your Preferences

On Facebook, you can adjust what you want to see in your timeline and what you do not want to see, and you can always hide people and posts that you are not interested in. However, if you want to make a bigger impact, make an attempt to change your preferences. You can select all your friends who you want to see first, reconnect with people you unfollowed in the past, and unfollow those who you don't want to be in touch with. You can make these adjustments by going to the Preferences menu of your News Feed and hover the cursor over the link at the left side of the screen. To the left of the words 'News Feed,' you will find an ellipsis icon, click it, and then select Edit Preferences option from the drop-down list. This will show you four options – Prioritize who to see first, Unfollow people to hide their posts, Reconnect with people you unfollowed, and Discover Pages that match your interests

Prioritize who to see first: This is an effective way of choosing people you want to see first in your feed – these can be your parents, your close relatives, your close friends, your siblings, your spouse and so on. Once you select these people, you will always see the posts from them at the top of your News Feed. These prioritized posts appear with a blue star, which distinguishes them from the normal posts.

Unfollow people to hide their posts: When you become friends with someone on Facebook, by default you start following them. This means their posts will appear in your News Feed, but if you do not want to see posts from some of your friends, you can always unfollow them. There could be several reasons why you might want to unfollow someone – he/she posts too frequently which spams your feed, you just don't like what he/she posts, or you do not want to know what that person is doing.

Reconnect with people you unfollowed: Someday you might want to reconnect with someone you had unfollowed in the past. You can always go back and reconnect with that person again by simply selecting their name from the list and adding them back on.

Discover Pages that match your interests: You might like certain pages and you might want to hear from them more often. You can have the posts from all such pages in your feed by just following them. Just open a Facebook Page and 'Like' it; this means you follow that page.

Keys to Facebook Advertising Success

Facebook advertising is incredibly effective and powerful, but it can't perform magic. You have to put in the right ingredients if you want to see great results. Some of the advertisers have unrealistic expectations that their ads will do wonders for them and drive enormous sales. But they must understand that, while Facebook is a powerful advertising tool, there are several reasons why it might not work for you. There are things that can make or break your advertising goals on Facebook.

Things that can break your advertising goals:

- **Your product**: If you shortlisted the product to be launched without doing enough research, and if no one wants to purchase it, your Facebook ads cannot conjure up sales.
- **Your brand**: Your product might be great and useful but it can be easily ignored by your audience if branding is not appropriate. This means branding is as important as the product itself. You need to spend enough time and money on branding, which includes a catchy logo, and impactful content.
- **Your website**: You might be redirecting all the traffic to your website, but if the website itself is badly designed and doesn't have meaningful content, the entire ad campaign will fail. Examples of broken websites could be that it does not have impactful content, it has broken links, or takes a long time to load.

These are some of the issues that can break your advertising campaign. Assuming you don't have any of these issues, look at the key reasons why your Facebook ads are not producing results.

Mistake 1: You are not reaching your target audience. This is the main reason why Facebook advertising doesn't work for some of the people. You are focusing on too broad an area, such as interests. For example, if you are focusing on interest targeting, interests are not as accurate as we think they are, and hence should not be considered as the focal point for targeting.

Mistake 2: You are targeting the right set of people but at the wrong time. For instance, interest targeting might work for top-of-the-funnel promotion and not for products. Similarly, targeting those who subscribed to your offering might work for selling and targeting those who landed on your website might be good to build your list by not yet for sales.

Mistake 3: You are targeting the right set of people at the right time, but not with the right messages. In such cases, ensure your message is impactful and polished so that it drives good results.

Mistake 4: Your budget is either too low or too high. The budget you set should be decided based on several factors so that it is just right for your campaign. If your budget is too high, your business might incur a loss. If the budget you set is too low, you might not be able to compete with your competition.

Mistake 5: Your bid is either too low or too high. Facebook sets automatic bidding by default – bidding that is important to reach those who might be interested in what you offer but for a lesser cost. Advertisers like to show their creativity here - not because the manual bids are not effective but because they like to make some adjustments based on some important factors that impact their business. However, they should always bear in mind that a bid too low can result in low distribution, which leads to reaching only the low-quality audience. Bids that are set too high can make you spend more than what is necessary.

Mistake 6: Your ads are optimized for actions that are not impactful. You should always look to optimize for conversions if that's what your ad objective is. If your ad objective is attracting more traffic, you must look to optimize the traffic, and similarly their engagement.

Mistake 7: You might be using the wrong ad type for your ad objective. Some of the advertisers complain that although they created a video for promoting their product, it didn't work for them and they didn't create conversions. The quality of their video might be great, but they failed to understand that they are probably not making an impact on the audience due to the wrong selection of the content type. The format should be in line with the ad objective. If the ad objective is getting video views, videos should be selected as the ad format. If the primary goal is to get more traffic to the website, using a link is important. When the objective is engagement, using an image makes it work. So, look at what you are trying to achieve from your ads and accordingly set the right ad format.

Mistake 8: You might not be experimenting enough to derive the results. If you are running ads for a new product or brand, experimenting is important as you might not know your audience immediately. You wouldn't know what works and what doesn't work. Therefore, experimenting and trying out different things until you know what works is important. If you have set up an ad campaign, created ad sets and also set up the ads, but didn't find success. You could run the same ads again or try something different. Experimentation and testing are needed because you cannot always be lucky to find success in the first go. You might have to try twice, three times or even more. Patience is the key. Never give up, and experiment.

Mistake 9: You might be focusing on the metrics that do not bring good results. Some of the advertisers are confused if they should focus on CMP, CTR, or CPC. Again, know your ad objective and see what metric would be right for your objective. For example – if your ad objective is conversion, then the metric you should be focusing on is Cost Per Conversion and not CTR or anything else.

Mistake 10: You might be tracking your performance, but not the right data. To be able to analyze the correct data, it is important that you install Facebook Pixel. If you do not, you might be in trouble as you wouldn't know if conversions are happening, and then you won't be able to optimize for the conversion.

These were the ten main reasons why your Facebook ads might not be working for you. You now need to look on the brighter side and see the elements that can bring success to your Facebook ads.

Right targeting is the most important thing that can make your campaign a big success. It was also at the top of the list of why your ads might not work, and for the same reason, it tops the list here also. This clearly shows that targeting is important for your ads as it can make or break your strategy. You might be able to come up with best ads for a quality product, but it won't matter if your ads are not targeting the right set of people. If you target people who are just not interested, there is no point of having these ads at all. The difference between targeting those who are interested in your offering and those who are a 'cold' audience is huge. This doesn't mean focusing on a cold audience is completely useless; you might succeed with them at a later time. The reality is you are more likely to find success in the marketplace if you target those who read what you write, who see what you post, who hear what you say. Spend as much time as you can to find out who is the target audience for you. If you do this well, you can lay a strong foundation for your advertising campaign on Facebook. Again – prioritize. You must prioritize your ad targeting.

- Website custom audience: this audience is the most powerful one as it captures people who are interested in what you do, and who visit your website. These are the people who sign up or register and also buy from you. Website custom audience also gives you the option to target according to factors, such as level of activity on your website, specific pages visited and so on. This can really boost your campaign.

Facebook Sales Funnel

Facebook is no longer just the coolest social media platforms on the busy web; it is no longer just another place for teens to share their updates with their friends; it is bigger than ever before. It is growing every day and is not likely to slow down in the near future. This is a good news for advertisers as the marketing opportunities it offers are immense. You can increase engagement with your potential customers, you can create and build brand awareness, you can make conversions, and increase sales. It all depends on what your ad objectives are and what you want to accomplish using this powerful platform. Facebook has more to do with socializing than anything else. In most cases, making a purchase would be the last thing on anybody's mind while browsing through the News Feed on Facebook, which means the possibility of selling on this platform is less. This is the reason why many brands become disappointed trying to sell their products on Facebook. They might be getting more engagement and more followers but still not be able to achieve their ad objective of increasing sales. The problem is not with the platform, it is the approach these advertisers take by trying to sell things to someone who might not even be interested. They should understand they cannot sell something to a user who doesn't have the purchasing mindset.

So, if you see an opportunity, it doesn't mean it is an opportunity to sell your product. This also doesn't mean that no one goes to Facebook with buying on their mind. Hence, you need to find the right set of people who might be interested in what you are offering. The best way of doing it is by developing a sales funnel.

Creating a Facebook Sales Funnel

Step #1: Create catchy and relevant content

To build a sales funnel, the first thing you need is different forms of content – video, blogs, webinars, ebooks, and so on. Different forms are required so that you can reach different types of audiences; some of them are more into watching the video, some like reading blog posts, so ensure you cater to different types of audiences. It is always good to have a good variety so that you have something for all sub-niche categories of your target audience. The content that you choose to put on your website to drive sales should be high quality and relevant to what you want to sell. Once your content reaches them, they are part of your funnel.

Step #2: Promote content to only those who are interested – a warm audience

Once you have the relevant content for your target audience, ensure it reaches the right set of people who are "warm". A warm audience means people who already know about you and your brand, and have shown some sort of interest in it. They can be your Facebook fans or a part of your website retargeting list. Regardless, ensure you engage with them and try to find out what is it that helps you make sales. Also, if you see that your warm audience is responding well to your content, there are chances that even a cold audience will. Therefore, analyze the data you get and see what's working and what's not.

Step #3: Do not forget to target your Lookalike Audience

Facebook gives you an opportunity to create Lookalike Audience – these are those who are very similar to your existing customers in terms of habits, interests, and behaviors. Hence, you can consider them as a cold audience who can be warmed easily since they look like the warm audience. To target them, navigate to the 'Audiences' section of your ads and then click on 'Create a Lookalike Audience'. You can find people who are similar to your most valuable targets. Select Source – which can be a Page, a conversion tracking Pixel or a Custom Audience. Next, select a Location and then Audience Size that can range anywhere from 1 to 10 percent of the total population in the locations you selected. Remember the smaller the percentage, the closer the match to your existing audience will be. Once done, click on 'Create Audience'.

Step #4: Advertise what is the best

The content that was most liked by your warm audience is the best content. You must take it to the cold audience to see if it can warm them too. The content can be in any form – it can be videos, blogs, or ebooks. The goal should be to move at least a part of the cold audience into your sales funnel so that they are aware of your brand. Only when they turn into a warm audience will they consider making a purchase. Without awareness, there cannot be a purchase.

Step #5: Consider remarketing to convert part of the cold audience into a warm audience

As we discussed previously, Facebook is more about socializing than purchasing. Most of the people are connecting with others and rarely do they consider making a purchase on this platform. This doesn't mean you cannot consider Facebook to help you in selling your products. With Facebook advertising, you cannot expect a cold audience to directly transform into qualified leads as this is not how it works on Facebook. Only when the cold audience is exposed to a brand multiple times, will they think about making a purchase. You can expose them to your brand several times so that they become a part of your funnel by remarketing.

Step #6: Using various options for remarketing

Utilize the power of Facebook Pixel: A powerful feature of Facebook advertising is Pixel that helps you remarket so that the user comes back to you to complete the purchase.

Use the power of visuals: Apart from Pixel, there are several other techniques that can be used for remarketing and one of the best ones is Videos. As we know visuals are more impactful, they can help you expose your brand to the audience.

Step #7: Create more warmth for your leads

With the help of remarketing, you could add some of your audience to the sales funnel. This is a great news but we need to do more than just this. This way you are only addressing a part of your audience as not everyone will convert. For example, perhaps some of the users visited your site and downloaded the free ebook but they never bought a copy from your website. To resolve this issue, create and run an ad to explain the benefits of what you are offering so that they are convinced.

Facebook Landing Page

The number of 'Likes' on your post and all the traffic you managed to generate with the help of News Feed ads are not worth much if you are not meeting the ad objective. To help you with this and to convert traffic into sales, advertisers are using a powerful marketing tool known as a Facebook Landing page. A Facebook Landing page is an independent webpage, which is standalone and not linked to the main navigation of your website. It is created so that users can take actions on your page. These actions could be signing up for your service, downloading a copy of your ebook, or buying the product from your website. Since it is designed in such a way to persuade the user to take an action, it is more convincing than any other page. But remember it is not just the design that attracts the users. To reap maximum benefits from the landing page, it should be in line with the advertising campaign it is part of, which means every promotion that you run would require its own unique page.

Why a business needs a landing page.

A landing page saves you from building your business on rented space. Think about where your business would be if Facebook and other social media platforms disappear tomorrow. Although it is very unlikely to happen if you are heavily dependent on a platform because your customers exist only there then your relationship with them is at stake. It is at the mercy of the next change in Facebook's working algorithm. Even if you don't think it this way, Facebook is a rented space and you do not own it the way you own your mailing list. By creating a landing page that gets all your fans onto the emailing lists, you have access to your customers beyond any social media platform. You can always connect with them and share updates about your new products through emails and add them to automated sequences to turn them into your potential customers. This way a Facebook Landing page offers you better opportunities to get your fans onto your emailing lists.

A landing page on Facebook can also help you achieve higher opt-in rates. The same landing page, when put on Facebook, is capable of earning more opt-ins. This is because people who visit your website do not know about you and there is less chance that they will respond to your lead generation campaigns. After all, people are not comfortable sharing their contact details with someone they do not know. On the other hand, they are well aware of Facebook and its credibility. They might even be seeing posts from you on a regular basis, and you might have even responded to some of their queries or comments on Facebook. So, they know your brand on Facebook and trust you enough to share their email address. Even if they have not interacted with you before, the element of trust attached to Facebook offers a certain level of credibility to your brand. Therefore, the landing pages get higher opt-in rates when they are published on a Facebook tab.

A Facebook Landing page is a perfect place to publish your ads. When the traffic is diverted to a Facebook tab, it is capable of achieving better approval rates. Hence, a landing page, when published on the custom Facebook tab, performs better.

Attributes of an Effective Facebook Landing Page

For a Facebook Landing page to be effective, it should have these attributes –

- **No Body, Footer or Outbound Links**. If there is nobody, footer or an outbound navigation link, it is difficult for a user to escape your website without converting. Instead of clicking on other tabs or links, he will remain focused on the Call-to-action. They do not have to leave the website to know more about you. Due to the same reasons, you should avoid having other pages, such as 'Careers', 'Contact Us' and so on. The logo on the page should take the users to the Home page. However, the focus for the user should be the Call-to-action.

- **A headline that speaks for itself**. Telling the world about the benefits your product offer isn't easy and that's why there are professionals who do this for business owners. The focus of the website and its design should always be such that the users know why they should approach you and how are you better than competitors. The first thing that appears on the landing page is the header. Therefore, ensure it is something that speaks to the benefits of your product.

- **A strong message that tells them they are in the right place**. Your landing page should have a strong message to the users that they are in the right place. It's the reason the Facebook Ad drives them to the landing page. This is called "message match" and is helpful in building trust with the user. The landing page's colors, headline, and everything else that the user sees should be in line with the ad.

- **Content that shows the benefits of the product**. Always bear your target audience in mind while you are curating content for your landing page. Remember that the readers are busy people and might not be interested in something that is complicated and sophisticated. They might not spend much time on your page. This is an opportunity to help them evaluate your offer. You might have an excellent vocabulary, but this is not the place to show off. Be as natural as possible so it sounds genuine. Don't get poetic - use bullet points to highlight the benefits of your product. Design it so it is easy for the user to skim through the content as that's all they can afford to do given the time limits. Note that bullet points are capable of enticing them to read what's given. If there is a long text, they might find the design too busy to read.

- **Visuals that help them connect with you**. Because visuals speak louder than words and are capable of conveying the underlying message efficiently and quickly, videos and images are always given preferences over text on the landing pages. These visuals are particularly useful in cases where a lot of information needs to be added – sales page and click-through landing pages. This is because explainer videos and infographics can effectively replace text that makes the pages content heavy. They also help the users understand your offering in a more effective and precise way.

- **Social proof yields more traffic**. Humans generally go by the recommendations of others who have tried something before. If there is good rating given to a hotel, we are more likely to try it. If there is always a queue outside a café, we assume it serves very good coffee. If your friend tells you that a particular movie is good, you'll want to see it. These are examples of social proof. You can use testimonials from your customers to prove that your product adds value. Buttons and widgets that provide information about the number of people who like your page can help users to know that your business has a good following. You can also showcase some of the things you have done in the past to boost traffic on your landing page. Buyers take cues from others. According to a survey conducted, approximately 88% of the users consider the online reviews of the product that other buyers have posted.

- **Catchy 'Call-to-action'.** The Call-to-action is the most important attribute of your landing page. Without this, a user cannot convert. Always include a button that is capable of getting the attention of visitors and motivate them to make purchase decisions. Also, the page should show the benefits of the offering over the features. For example – if the objective is to make people sign up for a class that can help them get a job in the foreign country, include an appropriate button. Do not include 'register' or 'download'. Try to use something that encourages them to click.

These features make your landing page effective, but there is always room for improvement on the first cut of your landing page. You can always learn new things that you can incorporate to make it even more efficient. For instance – the headline can be more optimized to resonate with the requirements of the users or the copy can be search engine optimized. One of the easiest and efficient ways to know that can be improved on your Facebook Landing page is the A/B method of testing.

A/B testing, also known as split testing, refers to a testing mechanism that compares two different landing pages at the same time – one is the 'A' version and another one is the 'B' version. Everything else remains the same including campaign run times, traffic sources and so on. It is a tactic by which you can find out which Call-to-action, ad headline, images, or body copy works best for your target audience. You can try out different ad placements and Facebook audiences to see which one is the perfect choice and where they are. There are two ways you can use the A/B to test your landing page.

One of the myths around A/B test is that you can only test one attribute at a time. For instance, to determine how effective the headline of the landing page is, you can compare the original page that has the headline to be tested against a variation of that page with a different heading. Whichever of these can attract and convert more visitors has the better and more effective headline.

This is the most accurate way to compare two pages, but it is certainly not the only one. Sometimes it is not possible to compare just one attribute at a time due to the test duration. That's why when a complete redesign of the page is needed there is a need to test multiple attributes at the same time. The variation page is compared with the original page in terms of form, headline, and even featured images. Once the complete test runs, the one that attracts a higher conversion wins because the ultimate goal of having a good landing page is to generate more conversions. Why it is better is not really important.

The steps involved in the A/B test.

Step 1: Collect Data to Be Analyzed

Test your landing page only when you have a reason. For testing, you can use your website or any of the several tools available in the market to determine how your Custom Audience is behaving. With the help of Google Analytics, you can see if your customers are abandoning the landing page without even visiting it. If it's happening, you need to discover the underlying cause and action on it immediately. For instance, if people are clicking on the navigation bar of your landing page instead of clicking the Call-to-action button, it is good to remove these kinds of distractions so that people focus on the Call-to-action. Try hiding the navigation button and now compare the page with the original page. You will see a boost in your conversions.

Step 2: Determine how many visitors you have to your page

You need to determine the number of visitors in a way that has statistical significance. This means you need to know how many visitors you need on each of your pages to be confident it is the genuine number and not happening by chance. Most of the industries have 95% as the accepted statistical significance, which means this percentage gives you confidence that the test results can be attributed to changes you made to the landing page.

Step 3: Develop Your Variation Page

The step involves making changes to your landing page based on the results of your A/B test – changes that will boost the conversion rate. For example, if it is determined that making changes to the headline can attract more visitors, you can create a new test page with the new headline. Also, if the results showed there is a need to add an image, create the variation page with the new headline and added image. All the changes you make as part of variation page shouldn't affect the control page. This is important because, without a baseline, you cannot compare the control page to understand how the variation page will perform.

Step 4: Test the new elements and the existing functionality

Before running the test, some of the things you must check are:

- The links are working fine and ads are directing you to the correct page
- The form is giving the right information to the CRM system
- When users click on CTA buttons, they are directed to the 'thank you' page
- The landing page looks correct in all the browsers

Step 5: Drive More Traffic to Your Landing Page

Once everything is tested, you can start generating traffic to your landing page. With Facebook, you can test traffic coming from different sources – News Feed ads, sidebar ads, audience network, and from different segments – females, males, singles etc., to evaluate the impact of traffic from these sources on your conversion rate. Remember that you shouldn't end the test before it reaches at least 95% statistical significance.

Step 6: Analyze the test results and improvise the landing page

Look at the results you have collected from various sources to see if the variation you created could achieve what you were looking for. If not, repeat the same process again, and keep testing and making changes till you see the desired results.

The Four Golden Rules of A/B Testing Ads:

Rule 1: Test only one attribute or variable at a time because of the fewer the variables, the more accurate the results. Testing just one variable per experiment makes tracking easier.

Rule 2: Use the correct campaign structure for your Facebook ads. You have two options: A single test set where all the ad variations are in a single ad set, and multiple single variation ad sets where each of the variations is part of separate ad set. If you place all the variations in a single set, you will not be able to see the relevant test results. Therefore, it is recommended that you should use the multiple single variation ad sets where all the variations are tested separately.

Rule 3: Make sure the test results from the split test are valid. You tested your campaign and you have your results now. To test the authenticity of your split test, you will have a good amount of result data. You can also use A/B

Significance Test to determine the authenticity of your test results.

Rule 4: Set a budget that is sufficient for the split test. You will need more advertising impressions as well as conversions if you are testing more ad variations. This will eat up your budget. Ensure you do not overdo it, but it should be just right so that you can get valid results.

Facebook Remarketing

Remarketing can be described as targeting the users who visited your website through an ad you had posted on Facebook. The platform gives advertisers an opportunity to show ads that resonate well with their content – whether it is about a blog post or about a product that they viewed. This requires creating ads and targeting website Custom Audiences.

The most important thing about advertising is targeting the right set of people, and remarketing helps you target those who showed interest in what you are offering. This is not the only factor that determines the success or failure of your ads, but it is by far the most important one. You can create the best copy with a great design and brilliant content, but if it doesn't reach the right set of people, what's the point of having the ad at all.

Many of the new advertisers experiment with different targeting options or groups of people but this is not always successful. For instance, by targeting people based on interests, you might not be able to reach the warm audience (people who know about your brand). In such cases, you are actually trying to sell something to people who don't even know you. But things are different in remarketing. Remarketing helps advertisers reach those who have shown interests in their offering at some time; they have revealed at least something about themselves by clicking on the advertiser's website. These actions are good enough to give advertisers an idea of what people are looking for, what they like and what their needs are. By reaching these warm audiences, you can expect a better response from your ads as these are about the brand they are already aware of.

Here are some of the ways advertisers reach out the warm audience through remarketing:

Consider those who clicked on your website:
We just defined remarketing that gives you the ability to reach out to those who visited your website. You can use Facebook Pixel to generate audiences based on pages the users visited. Remarketing with Website Custom Audiences helps you reach out to:

- People who visited specific web pages
- People who visited your website
- People who clicked on some web pages but not others
- People who haven't visited your website over a span of time

The data that is collected using these parameters is crucial. By targeting those who have visited your website, you can promote your content in the hopes of receiving positive responses. By targeting people who visited only some web pages, you can determine the audience who read specific blogs. By targeting people who visited specific web pages but not others, you can determine the ones who reached your website but didn't convert. By targeting people who haven't visited over a span of time, you can try doing something that can re-engage them.

Facebook also provides you 'Advanced Mode' for retargeting that helps you create audiences who viewed your website multiple times in last 180 days, or made a purchase, or made a purchase of at least $20, or searched for a specific website at least once.

This is great for advertisers who own a website. In the event that you do not have a website, or you have a light-trafficked website, you have options.

Those who viewed your video: Those who watch your video seem to be interested in your business. You can always consider retargeting this group of viewers as they showed interest in their action. Advertisers can consider creating an audience if people:

- Watched your video for at least 3 seconds
- Watched your video for at least 10 seconds
- Watched at least 25% of your video
- Watched at least 50% of your video
- Watched at least 75% of your video
- Watched at least 90% of your video

Using this method, you can also determine the more relevant audiences as those who watched your video for longer durations are more interested in your business.

Those who opened the Lead Ad form: These Lead Ads allow the users remain on Facebook instead of redirecting them to different landing pages. By creating Custom Audience for these Lead Ads, advertisers can build an audience by determining who opened the form and submitted, who only opened the form but didn't submit, and those who only opened the form. By determining those who opened the form and submitted, you can determine who can be targeted. By determining those who only opened, you can see those who are interested in your offering. By determining those who opened but never submitted, you can see who to exclude.

Those who interacted with your page: you can target those who engaged with your page content by determining:

- Who engaged with your page
- Who visited your page
- Who engaged with your post or ad
- Who clicked any Call-to-action button
- Who sent a message to your page
- Who saved any post or page

To find the biggest audience, attempt to target those who engaged with your page.

Chapter 3:

Creating a Facebook Business Page

Facebook Business Page offers exciting opportunities for promoting and advertising your business. It doesn't matter whether you are trying to advertise your online business or a brick-and-mortar shop, your Business Page will help you improve your visibility.

Some people believe that they just need a personal profile on Facebook and activate the subscribe button. Hence, they don't need a Business Page. Creating a Facebook Profile and then creating a Facebook Business Page has its own beauty. When you create a personal profile, you can be connected to only certain people. When you create a Business Page, you can be connected to as many people as you want; there is no limit on the number of likes (number of fans) you can have on your page. With a Business Page, you can integrate several apps that are useful to your business to help you engage and connect with more users, such as newsletter sign-ups, live chats, etc.

So, now you are convinced and all set to create your Business Page on Facebook. There are steps to set up your page for success and take advantage of what Facebook has for you and your business. Remember, your Business Page will be attached to your Facebook profile so that users will know who owns it, but it is a separate presence that you can use to promote your brand, product, service, or business.

Facebook has been constantly trying to make its business pages as defined and broad as possible. A Business Page can be created for:

- A local business or place
- An organization, company or institution
- An artist, band or public figure
- A brand or product
- A cause or topic
- Entertainment

1. **Local Business or place** – There are several business owners who simply choose this option as it says "local business" but this is wrong. This category is not appropriate for all types of businesses; it is good only for certain kinds of businesses. For example, if you have a physical location from which to operate, this category works the best for you. If you work from home, you can choose this category and then treat it as your home office. But it doesn't solve the problem if someone wants to come to your office. This is what happens. When you select the category Local Business, Facebook gives you an option to select a sub-category. You can select one from a huge list. If you don't find an appropriate one, you can select the 'generic' type from the list given. Once you choose this, you are asked to fill in the complete details of your business, which helps people find you easily using Search Engine Optimization (SEO) and Google Plus.

2. **Organization, company, or institution** – This is the category that works well for those businesses that operate online. It is also the right option for those who

have multiple work locations, such as a business with multiple branches within a city or in different cities. Once you select this category, Facebook will ask you to choose a sub-category from the long list. Select one that matches the requirement that you do not sell your services or products through physical stores.

3. **Artist, Band or Public Figure** – This category works for public figures, musicians, artists, entrepreneurs, or authors. This is the category that emphasizes promoting the individual rather than the business. If you are an artist or an entrepreneur who has multiple jobs, you can use this category to promote yourself and what you do. This page type is the best alternative for having a personal profile as an author, businessman, or a single person.

4. **Brand or Product** – This category is meant for those businesses that want to advertise their brand or sell a product without specifically advertising their products. For instance, LG can create a brand page that focuses on LG Electronics, or even for the overall LG brand. They can also choose to create specific product pages for advertising the new products of LG. Once you select this category, it will ask you to select the sub-category for your brand or product, such as electronics or home décor.

5. **Cause or topic** – This is the category for non-profits. If you want to create a page on Facebook for a cause or community, this is the category you should select. For example, if you are a group that conducts events for charity purposes, select the category 'Cause or Topic'.

6. Entertainment – This category is meant for entertainment purposes and less for business. If you conduct events or entertainment related shows, your page should be the 'Entertainment' category. For instance, to advertise your new album as a brand, create a page with the category 'entertainment'. If you are on Facebook to entertain your target audience, and not for any other purpose, this is the right choice for you.

If you are not sure which of these categories to select, you certainly have a default option of creating a Facebook personal profile, which is much simpler and easier to manage as compared to the Facebook Pages. You must compare the features and benefits of each. Facebook Personal Profile might be simple to create and manage, but it doesn't have some of the important features that a Facebook Page has, which includes different ways of networking, and advertising, insights.

A profile works well in some instance, and sometimes a page should be created.

A personal profile comes in handy when you are looking for something for personal use – with a casual tone. It can be used for professional things and it can be an alternative to a Page of a public figure. If you are looking at just the basic features of Facebook and not interested in the advanced features, networking options, apps, and other tools, you can choose a personal profile instead of a Page.

If you want to utilize the power of some of the advanced features of Facebook for networking your business or to access the detailed insights or run an ad campaign to promote your business, having a Facebook Page is important to use. You will need the Page version if you are anything other than the single entrepreneur. According to the rules and regulations of Facebook, you cannot use your personal profile for business purposes, and this is reflected in various places. For instance, you cannot create tab applications using your personal profile as there is no way to display them. From your personal profile, you can follow pages, but you cannot send a personal note to anyone without having received one first as this is considered unsolicited. At any given point in time, you can have just one personal profile, but you can have as many Pages as you want. If you are an entrepreneur who hosts events, develops products and owns two businesses, you can create your own personal profile, a Page of 'entertainment', a Page of 'product', and two business Pages. This way you have more options than just creating a personal profile and trying to achieve everything from it.

You now understand the need of having Facebook Pages and appreciate what it does for you and your business. However, if you create a page and later feel you do not actually need it and that it's limiting your actions, Facebook allows you to convert your page to a personal profile. We will see how to achieve this later in this chapter.

Creating a Business Page

Step 1: Choose the Right Type

To be able to create a Business Page on Facebook, you first need to log into your personal profile and browse through the Home page. Once you are there, go to the Explore section displayed on the left-hand sidebar of your profile page. Next, click on Pages tab and it will take you to the main Pages section. As you explore this section, you will see suggestions, invites to other users, pages you have liked, pages you are managing, and an option to create a new page. Click on Create Page. It will then ask you the type of Business Page you want to create. Choose from the six categories we discussed earlier. Each of these types has a drop-down menu with many options for that selected page type.

You might not be able to judge the importance of selecting the right page type for your Business Page, but when you look at the exhaustive sub-categories listed under each of these categories, you will appreciate the importance of each of the page types provided by Facebook. Then you will be able to find the perfect category for your business type. Remember that each of the page types brings along with it a set of unique category options, and each of these options, in turn, has its own unique characteristics. Therefore, don't rush to select the page type. Analyze, think carefully, read all the sub-categories and the characteristics of each, and then make your choice.

Once you have decided on the Page type, select the category from the drop-down list of that page type to choose the best option. if you are not happy with what you have selected after the page is live, you can always go back to the categories and change it to something more appropriate.

Next, you will enter the new Business Page you have created, along with few other details required to get started. Enter the name and the required details to proceed. Remember the name you give to your Business Page is a unique identifier that will identify your business. The name should be well-thought and should be something that clearly defines what you or your business stands for. This means it should be closely related to your business or brand name.

Add the description of your business. Pay attention to what you write as this will impact your business. Try to make it search engine optimized as doing so will help you get listed when someone searches for something related to your business or brand. You can use up to 155 characters to describe what you do, so try to be as descriptive as possible. Remember, is it something that will appear near the top of your business profile on both desktop and mobile sites.

Do not forget to enter the URL for your page and ensure that you enter is correct. This is important as people will click on it to get in touch with you.

When you are entering the details, you will be prompted with a list of ideas and tips designed to help you create an impactful Business Page before you start inviting your friends to like it. Take a look at these tips as some of them might come in handy.

At this point, you might want to unpublish your page as you are still in the process of setting it up. So, browse through the top navigation button and click on Settings. Click on General Settings and then open the Page Visibility section. You will be able to see two options – click on Page unpublished and save the changes. You can now proceed and build your page offline and publish it later once you are finished.

Step 2: Upload a Profile Picture

The next step is to design and upload a profile picture that draws the users' attention to your page. You can use various ideas to design a profile picture, such as a picture of your product or the logo/images associated with your brand or business (street sign or image of the store). You can even choose one of your pictures if you are the face of the business. Remember to keep the composition simple so that the user can see it clearly as it is this picture that will appear every time you publish a post or comment on someone else's post. It will uniquely identify you and your business. Use square dimensions as rectangular ones are normally cropped to squares by Facebook. The specifications for your profile image as it will be viewed in various places:

- Profile picture on the main page – 160 x 160
- In your timeline – 86 x 86
- In News Feed – 100 x 100
- Icon when you comment – 43 x 43

Keep these sizes in mind and select an image accordingly. Once you are ready, upload it on your Business Page by clicking on Add a Picture. You will be given the options to either take a photo using the camera of your computer or upload an image saved on your computer. Just follow the instructions and upload the selected image.

Step 3: Add a Cover Image

Using the same process with different dimensions, upload the cover image. The dimensions of the cover picture are 828 x 315 pixels. Always remember that the picture should be visually attractive, must represent your business, and should have great quality. Another thing to keep in mind is that dimensions for mobile devices are 560 x 315 pixels.

Once you are ready with an image, consider the dimensions for mobile as well as the desktop website, browse through the upper-left corner of the Cover Photo section and click on Add a Cover. Now click on Upload Photo option and save the changes. Once the image is uploaded, click on the photo to edit it. Fill in the description as this is an important part of your page. You can either share a tagline that describes your business or include a link to your landing page. Utilize this description and try to make it search engine optimized.

Step 4: Include a Call-to-Action

The Call-to-Action button enables your viewers to do certain things easily when viewing your page. They can like it, share your page, buy something, or signup for a newsletter. Browse through the right corner of the cover image and click on Add a button. Upon clicking, you will be given a choice of the following types of buttons:

- **Book services**: This button has two options- Book Now (the user canto book your time for something you are offering), and Start Order (people can order products from you).
- **Get in Touch**: This button has five options – Call Now (the user can call you using single click option), Contact Us, Sign Up (takes the user to a form for lead generation), Send Message (the user can send you a private message using the Facebook chat window) and Send Email (the user can send you an email message with one click option).
- **Learn More**: This button has two options – Watch Video (takes the user to your website to watch a video) and Learn More (shows extra information about you and your business to the user).
- **Make a Purchase/Donation**: This is a single button – Shop Now allows the user to buy your product or service on your Business Page or website.

- **Download App or Game**: This has two options – Use App (takes the user to the app directly and hence helps in engagement) and Play Game (the user can download/play the game).

You can explore all the options provided by Facebook to find which one best fits your business.

Step 5: Add Other Information

The next step is to add additional details about your business, such as Business Hours, website link etc.

Step 6: Adjust Privacy and Security Settings

You have entered all the required details on your page. Now it is time to make it secure by defining the access and roles you will give to different people. This will help you organize how users can reach and engage with you.

General Settings: Some of the helpful settings from the General Settings section are:

Enable Shortcuts so that Facebook pins your page to shortcut. This will save a few steps to navigate to the Business Page and provide quick access to it.

Regarding Visible Posts, select Anyone can publish posts, photos, and videos to your page. Do not worry about what content others will post on your page as you can always review the content and approve or reject the post before it is published on your page.

Give others the ability to get in touch with you by asking questions through Facebook Messenger. As this improves engagement, enable this option by ticking the option that displays the message button on your Business Page.

Others can Tag your page and Share it as it is an effective way to reach an audience and extend your network. Reap benefits from this option by ticking the Others Tagging this Page.

If you deal with industries that are age-sensitive, such as tobacco, it will be good to Restrict the page to certain age groups. The Age Restrictions offers six different options to choose from.

You can also Block Comments that contain certain words you have selected or defined. This can be achieved using the Page Moderation settings that have different kinds of profanity filters.

You can also Post in Multiple Languages if your audience is spread across the globe or is multi-lingual. By ticking this options, your posts will be displayed to your audience in multiple languages.

Messaging Settings: When someone messages you privately through your Business Page, Facebook provides you an option to deliver automated responses by turning on the response assistant. Your automated response will be personalized as it will contain your name; you can even edit the template to match your style. You can send an auto-response in cases when you want to thank your user for getting in touch with you, so they know you have received their message but are busy right now, and to confirm that you have received their message and you are working on their request.

Page Settings: You can edit the Business Page settings to customize the selection of tabs that are displayed in the left pane of the page. Click on Edit Page settings and click-drag each tab that you want to see there.

Notification Settings: allows you to select how you want to be notified whenever there is an activity on your Business Page - each time something happens or only once in 24 hours, the type of activities you want to be notified about, each time someone likes your page, each time someone shares your post. You can turn these settings on and off.

Your Business Page is now ready. It is time to publish it so that the world can see it. Remember you had unsubscribed the publish button to work offline till you set it up. Change it back to Publish, and Get-Set-Go!

Engage and Manage your Business Page

You might be quite excited to share your Business Page with your connections the moment you create it, but hold on and control your temptations. Take a moment to think about your strategic plan and seed your Business Page with relevant and engaging content so that people do not have any other option but to stop by. The content on your Business Page should be highly engaging and inviting.

It is important that you stay connected with your readers and publish posts every now and then. Create a schedule to publish these posts after analyzing various factors, such as on which days of the week should these posts be published, what time of the day are the target customers most active on social channels, what topics should be chosen, etc.

In simple terms, there are three types of posts that you can publish on your Facebook Page:

- Content update
- Photos and/or videos
- Links

According to studies conducted, content that has photos are capable of garnering 2-3 times more engagement than content shared without images. Ensure you make visuals an important part of your Facebook advertising strategy.

Regarding frequency, there is no hard and fast rule. The changes in the algorithms Facebook uses has made it difficult to research the subject. The majority of people seem to be experimenting with frequency. When they see a pattern, which seems to be working out for their posts, they adopt it. I would recommend you do the same thing. See what frequency works for you and analyze the results to see the impact.

However, there is something you must be consistent with – your content. if your content is engaging and interests the readers, they will expect you to post on regular basis. Do not disappoint them. Once a schedule works out for you, stick to it. You can also make use of different apps, such as Buffer that will make the entire task of scheduling easier. All you need to do is keep the content ready and add the posts to the queue and the app will do the rest. It will ensure your page always has engaging and fresh content and will post it automatically as per the schedule created. Also, use Facebook Insights (which I will discuss later in this ebook) to determine what works and what does not.

When you are sharing the page for the first time, share your Business Page with your connections only after publishing 3-4 posts on it so that you have some engaging content. Once you have content ready on your page, try out some of the following strategies to get your first fans.

Invite Facebook Friends

Facebook has an inbuilt feature to tell your Facebook friends about your Business Page. So, utilize this feature and share the good news. Go to the top right corner of your page and click on the Build Audience link. You can then select your Facebook friends by clicking on Invite Friends option from the drop-down menu. You also have an option to search your friends based on lists, groups, recent conversations, location etc. Once the invite is sent, your friends will receive the invite message as a notification. They can now like and see your Business Page. You can also ask your co-workers to like the page you just created. Ask them to recommend the page to their connections who might be interested in what you are offering.

Promote on Your Website

To promote your Business Page on your website, Facebook offers you a complete gamut of buttons and widgets that can be easily added to your website so that visitors can easily act on it by either liking or sharing with their connections.

One of the most exciting plugins offered by Facebook is the Facebook Page plugin. Using this plugin, you can embed your Business Page on your website and promote it without your visitors having to leave your site the same way they can share and like the page without leaving your website.

Promote in Your Email Signature

One of the creative ways to promote your Business Page is through your emails. Your inbox has one of the most visible ways to promote your page. Include the link to your Business Page in your email signature and add it as a Call-to-action in your emails.

Organize Contests

Facebook contests are becoming increasingly popular. They can act as a promotion tool to drive more traffic to your Business Page. There are several apps available to create these contests including Gleam and ShortStack.

Try out these strategies to see which one works the best for you.

Administering your Facebook Page

When you are trying to be as active as you can on your Facebook Business Page, you often want to do a lot of things at the same time. Administering your page is not easy and it can be really tedious to keep a track of all the different things you are doing. Monitoring your activities is important as you need to understand if your hard work and time are being used efficiently. The best possible solution to deal with this is to have a notification mechanism that will monitor your activities and tasks for you. If you check manually, you might miss a few things including your posts and messages. Then your ranking goes down and your engagement with your target audience also drops. This will result in lower sales and less traffic on your website. Here are a few options to set up alerts and notifications:

Facebook's Native Notifications

Facebook offers its users a native system that can send alerts and notifications for a Facebook Page. This service can be activated by logging in to the page and clicking on the Settings menu. In settings, select Notifications to see the different options available. You will be provided with four different ways for delivering notifications: On Facebook, Text messages, Email, and Messages.

On Facebook: This is the typical notifications on Facebook that you often get when someone leaves a comment on a post or when a page you are following has a post published on it. These notifications can be found in the top bar of your page. To see these notifications, you have to log into your Facebook account and manually go to the Notifications tab. When a number appears on the top notifications tab, you have a message. Facebook also highlights it by dynamically changing the meta title of the page from "Facebook" to "(1) Facebook". When you check this update, this number will disappear and it will appear again only when there is another notification alert. This way you can passively monitor the notifications on Facebook. This depends on two things: you always have to have your Facebook desktop site open and the code that is active on Facebook. If the scripts are slow, or if you get multiple notifications at the same time, you might be able to monitor it effectively.

Notifications via Emails: This is one of the best ways to have timely updates. Email notifications will send you messages via emails whenever there is something happening on your Facebook Page. If someone comments on your post or shares it with another user, you will receive an email alert. You can choose to set up email filters so that the other normal emails are filtered out, and only the important emails about comments on your post or messages are sent to notify you. This method of receiving notification is quite effective.

Notifications using the Text Messages: This method will send text messages to the user whenever there is an important activity on the page. However, if you own large Facebook pages with lots of engagement activities and notifications flowing in, it might be cumbersome for your phone.

Notifications using Messages: You will receive a notification whenever you are sent a message on your page. But when there is a notification, you do not receive any message. You can choose to go with this option to respond to your customer's messages, but keep it in mind that it doesn't handle notifications.

There are three main settings, out of which one is not turned on. The ones that are on receive a notification whenever there is an important update or any new activity, or one notification with details of all the activities that happened in that day. The second option is generally not considered by small players as they should respond to the customer's requests quickly and not after a delay of 20-24 hours. However, this method works out if you have larger pages with lots of notifications. You can have a dedicated resource to constantly monitor the activities including the messages and comments. You can also turn the notifications on or off for specific types of interaction, such as new reviews, new shares on the post, new comments on the post, new followers of the page, edits to the posts, edits to the comments, new likes, new likes on a page, or new subscribers to an event you have created.

Converting a Page to a Profile and a Profile to a Page

There used to be no connection between Pages and Personal Profiles and pages were not different from the profiles; they were just personal profiles with some additional attributes. Therefore, there was a lot of confusion as to what to use – a personal profile or a page. People needed clarity so that they can create the right entity considering the needs of their business.

Today, after various upgrades and optimizations applied by Facebook, people can see the difference between a personal profile and a page. However, there is still a common issue. Some of the personal Facebook users feel the need to change their page to a personal profile so that they can use the basic features of a profile. Some business owners who have profiles see these profiles limiting their abilities and want to convert their profiles to a Business Page.

If you are using your profile to promote your business, you need to stop as this is not allowed by Facebook and it is against their terms and conditions. If they catch you using your personal profile for business purposes, they will either force you to convert it into a page, or they will delete your account. Pages do not have the organic reach that personal profiles do due to a number of friends that can be added to the profile. Just having good organic reach is not the ultimate goal of Facebook marketing. Having access to numerous marketing and insight tools, and targeting options are also important. All these features are available free to all Pages irrespective of their type and size. Both Pages and Profiles are available for free and are fun to create. There will be a cost only when you want additional options for advertising.

The process of conversion is quite easy and all you need to do is to browse through the Profile to Page Migration option. You will need to enter the category of your new Page (which you are converting to) as well as the sub-category based on your requirements. Once you enter the category and sub-category, you might be asked to enter some more information. However, before you complete the conversion process, determine if you are the admin of any of the groups on your profile. If you are, you will lose access to those groups once the profile is converted to the Page. Some of the information will be transferred and saved to your new Page. For instance, all your existing friends will be transferred and saved as followers on your Business Page. Whatever you had uploaded as your profile pictures becomes your Page profile picture, and the username of your profile becomes the username of your Business Page. If you were managing any pages, you will still continue to do so. Also, you need to download other information, such as messages and posts before you begin the conversion. So, the two things that you need to take care of before starting the conversion process are your admin rights and your content.

You can also convert a Business Page to a Personal Profile. Although it is not as simple as the other process, if you understand the concept and underlying idea, you can do it. The first step is to raise a request to convert your Page to a Personal Profile while you are logged in to your Business Page. This request is raised by filling out a form that goes directly to Facebook. Once received, Facebook verifies the details, reviews your request, and analyzes if the conversion is possible. Make sure you provide a good reason why you want to convert your Page to a Profile, as if they reject the request, you might not get a second chance.

If Facebook feels that your Page is being used for business purposes, it might not allow you to convert it into a Profile. There are two cases in which they are likely to approve your request:

- You had a profile but, by mistake, you converted it into a page.
- Facebook forced you to convert your Personal Profile to a Page under the mistaken impression that you were using your Personal Profile for business operations. If you can prove that you weren't and that they were a mistake, you can convert it to a Personal Profile again.

There may be times that you do not hear from Facebook about your request. This doesn't mean they have rejected your request. It could be that they haven't yet had time to look into your request. Get in touch with them directly.

Chapter 4:

The Impactful Facebook Ads

According to studies conducted, more than 95% of social media advertisers think Facebook is the most effective social media platform for advertising purposes. In recent years, social media has grown to be a highly popular advertising platform. The main reason is that it is one of the most effective advertising channels that help businesses get new leads and turn them into potential clients.

Facebook ads are effective for both types of organizations - B2B and B2C. There are so many stories that relate remarkable increases in marketing results after adopting Facebook advertising as their marketing strategy. It's never too late to adopt Facebook advertising as your marketing weapon as there has been a constant growth in both advertising opportunities offered by Facebook.

Setting up ads on Facebook is really simple and you can realize fast results. If you compare it without other social media channels, you will see that creating Facebook ads is significantly simpler. You need not spend hours on learning about it. Moreover, you don't even need to spend thousands of dollars to advertise on this social platform.

Another reason for advertising on Facebook is you can reach your target audience effectively. According to statistics, there are billions of people who see an ad through social channels every month. Out of millions of Facebook users, an average person spends around 45-50 minutes daily on these social channels – Facebook, Instagram, Twitter etc. These figures indicate there are new opportunities for your business to reach a multitude of users. With Facebook, you can customize a target audience making it possible for advertisers to target their customers based on variables, such as location, demographics, age, engagement and so on. This makes it the best advertising medium to create target audiences to produce high returns.

You now have enough reasons to create your ads on Facebook. So, now you can create your first ad.

Ingredients Needed to Create a Facebook Ad

To create an ad on Facebook, you need:

- A business goal for running the ad
- Defining your target audience to describe who you want to reach
- Decide the ad placement
- Setting a Daily or Lifetime budget for your ad
- The format - how should you tell your story

Choose your Business Goal

Choosing a goal is important because Facebook advertisements are quite versatile and you can see the real value of those ads when you are focused on what exactly you want to achieve.

Your business goal can be anything from increased brand awareness to driving more sales or increasing downloads of the app you have embedded in your Business Page. Goals are categorized under three headings: awareness, engagement, and conversion.

Awareness – when you want people to notice you/your business. If your goal is to get people to notice you, it's time to put what you do on their radar; it is time to raise awareness. Introduce them to your product or business. Advertising on Facebook for brand awareness helps you reach and connect with more people who might be interested in what you are doing. Get their attention through your ads. It's easy to increase your brand awareness through social channels such as Facebook where millions of people are waiting to discover new things. Engage them in visual advertisements and show them something really intriguing. Give them ads that become the best indicators of your brand and the best indicators of what you do. Facebook achieves this and builds your brand by optimizing your ads, which in turn improves the reach.

Optimization Options:

➤ Brand awareness
➤ Reach

Supported Ad Formats:

➤ Single Image
➤ Single Video
➤ Carousel
➤ Slideshow
➤ Canvas

Engagement – You need to engage the people you know so that they become potential customers. You need to give them something to learn, something they can follow and explore. Why not improve your engagement with your target audience through app installs, website clicks, page posts, video views, lead generation etc.

Engage with more and more people and get them download your app because these mobile apps play a key role in improving the reach of your business and help engage the users. The App Install ads are shown on Facebook and are linked directly to several sites such as Google Play for people to download easily.

Engage more people through website click ads. This way you can drive more traffic to your Business Page to promote your product or business. Think about where you want to direct the users when they click on your ad on Facebook. Once this is decided, you can upload images, add descriptions and headlines, and include a Call-to-action button to persuade people to do what you want them to do.

The App Engagement ads are designed to increase actions through engagement in the mobile applications. You can reach out to people who use mobile applications extensively, so there is a good chance to encourage them to take actions and come back to you for several things such as booking their travel, shopping etc. It is possible to direct people to specific sections of the application. You can reconnect with your old customers who used the app before, encourage people to play, shop, or book their travels, and grow their business.

Facebook's Lead Generation Ads make it easy for others to know and learn about what you do while you generate leads. You might not realize there are several people who are interested in your business and want to hear back from you, but getting the information by filling in forms could be tedious and time-consuming. That's where most lose interest and don't even get in touch with you. Facebook is here to help you with this. The Lead Ads on Facebook has made the lead generation process very simple. With these ads, when someone taps on the ad, a form pops up with some information already published. Facebook uses its intelligence to pre-populate the fields using the contact information users upload on the platform without worrying about filling the time-consuming forms, and you get the generated lead.

Facebook's Page Post Engagement Ads tell people about what you do so that they can take the required action. You can reach out to new people and remain connected with existing ones. The ads help you share information about your business with the customers in an effective manner. These Page Post Engagement ads also help you understand the type of content your target audience prefers and likes with the help of insights, such as how many people commented or liked your ad, how many shared it in their network etc. Once you know what they like and what they are looking for, you can create more of the same.

The Event Response Ads aim to reach people who are interested and are likely to attend your event. All you need to do is create an event from your page and share it with others to spread the message through these ads to make your event a success. You can select the audience that might be interested in your event. When someone asks to join the event, it is automatically added to their Facebook calendar. The ad should be displayed to all those who might be interested in your event. Invite them and offer them a way to join. You can divert them to the website or app to buy tickets. You can also see the number of invitees so you can keep track of how many people respond to your invitation.

The Offer Ads help you extend offers to attract people. Offering a good discount or a special deal is a sure shot solution to get the attention of customers. When you wish to increase your sales, whether it is online or in your store, get their attention and encourage them to take actions on the discounts and promotions. To make the job simpler, Facebook ads help you create these discounts and promotions easily and they can be customized to match your needs.

Facebook Video ads can engage communities of people who are active on Facebook and who love watching videos. People are spending more than 100 million hours on Facebook watching videos. Videos are always better than just text and they are more effective. So, create an effective video and create an ad around it.

Engage your customers through Messages. Facebook has an option for you to have open conversations with your customers to drive results. The message ads give you the opportunity to interact more personally with your customers to increase sales, drive leads, and respond to queries. When people "message" you, you know they are interested. You can drive results faster and better by helping your customers complete their purchase transactions in the message thread itself.

Optimization Options:

> Impression
> Daily unique reach
> Post Engagement

Supported Ad Formats:

> Single Image

- Single Video
- Carousel
- Slideshow

Conversion – Once you have gained the confidence of your fans, you can nudge them to buy your product or sign up for services. This is what is called conversion. Facebook makes conversion an easy process with the help of its Advertising strategy.

Use Facebook Website Conversion ad objective to persuade people to take action on your website. You can grow sales by helping people complete transactions on your website, or prompt them to do something you want them to do – visit your site, add something to their cart etc. You can also increase traffic by visiting a specific page or exploring the website.

If the ad objective is conversion, you can also utilize the power of Dynamic Ads on Facebook. These Dynamic Ads allow you to personalize your ads. Facebook will promote your business or products to those who are interested in your business or have shown an interest by visiting your website or using the app. All you need to do is upload your product catalog and set up the campaign for just one time, and the magic will happen. The ad will continue to work for as long as you want, which means it will continue to find people for each of the products in the catalog and always apply the updated price and availability for the product. This way you can reach out to more shoppers by showing them products they are interested in, complete the sale by retargeting these interested shoppers, remind them to buy things they had reviewed but not bought, and connect with them across the devices by contacting them wherever they had originally shopped.

Optimization Options:

- ➢ Conversions
- ➢ Reach
- ➢ Impressions
- ➢ Link Clicks

Supported Ad Formats:

- ➢ Single Image
- ➢ Single Video
- ➢ Carousel
- ➢ Slideshow
- ➢ Canvas
- ➢ Collection

Dynamic ads have several benefits over conventional ads. Facebook always focuses on how to make the platform a better place to increase engagement. In this quest, it came up with the concept of Dynamic Ads that are designed particularly for those who have various significant product catalogs. These ads are great with what they can do for multiple products. When you include metadata in your product pages similar to the schema by flagging important data, such as product name, image, and price, Facebook creates multiple ads using this data. Facebook also analyzes the data of the individual products in your catalog and targets people using those products that these people might be looking for. For example, a general store that sells everything from grocery and food items to drinks to branded products. If they want to advertise one of these categories to their entire target audience, it is likely to have low conversion as not everyone who visits the store will buy the items in this category. For such a store, it is difficult to build a focused target audience. If they start promoting all their brands or products, it is going to be insane looking at the number of items they have.

This is where Dynamic Ads are used. They handle such scenarios by picking data from the product pages and creating multiple ads. This way you can handle a huge number of ads without actually creating them. This is the power of Dynamic Ads.

Drive conversions through store visits. Some facts:

- Even today, around 90% of the retail purchases happen offline in the US
- Around 56% of the store purchases are impacted by the digital influence
- Only a small fraction of people use the Facebook app at the time of shopping in a store

If the objective of your Facebook Ad is to encourage more people to visit your shops, utilize the Facebook Store Visits ads to help you bridge the gap between the online and offline shopping experiences of these people. This will generate more store visits and sales at the brick-and-mortar shops. Facebook will help you localize your message so that your customers receive personalized texts or map cards created specifically for your business location near them. These messages will include the complete address and other contact details. It will help them locate you easily by directing them to the nearest shop. People will also be prompted to action offline with the help of CTAs that help drive offline results.

Connect your offline data to Facebook and it becomes conversions to allow you to utilize your offline data from qualified leads, over-the-phone bookings etc., to power your digital campaigns. You just need to connect the CRM or any other system that holds the offline data to your account to keep track of events that are not available online. This way you can measure conversions happening across the channels and create Custom Audiences from Offline Events.

Creating Custom Audience for Offline Events

Facebook recently considered adding the ability for offline businesses to track the impact of the ads they publish with Offline Event Sets. Using this feature, marketers can now target their audience using Offline Event Custom Audience. Before we get into the details, it is important to understand how to create these Offline Event Sets.

Navigate to Offline Events within your Ads Manager and then select a data source for the Offline Event Set. Give an appropriate name and description, and click on 'Create'. Note that this Offline Event set has been created for one of your ads and you have also gathered data from your offline sales. Upload these details on the Create Offline Event set. Your data file can have up to six columns for event descriptions, such as Event Name, Time, Currency, Order Id and so on, and 17 identifiers, such as First Name, Last Name, Email, Mobile Number, Age, Gender, City, State, Country and so on.

To understand this: You publish an ad on Facebook and it was shown to your audience. Some of them click or saw this ad, and some of these visited your offline store. Now, you need to furnish the details on Facebook about all those who clicked or saw the ad and then visited your offline store. You should have the details in the files, such as Event, Date and time of purchase, First name, Last name, order ID, email address/contact details, value. Using this information,

Facebook can analyze how many visited the store and made a purchase vs. how many saw/clicked on the ad. With this offline data, you can create your target audience using the methods described below.

To Create an Offline Event Custom Audience:

Method 1: From the top right corner of the screen, click on 'Create Audience' and from the drop-down menu, select 'Custom Audience'. In the new screen that opens up, select your ad account for the Custom Audience. To set the Audience Type, select from the four options that appear in the menu – Everyone in the event set, People based on total purchase value over time, People associated with a specific event type and People with custom attributes. If you select 'Everyone in the event set', you are actually converting the entire file into a Custom Audience set, whether the people in the set clicked or saw your ad or not. If you select 'People based on total purchase value over time', you can mention the value that you want to set the limit. By default, Facebook sets it to 'Total purchase value is greater than or equal to 100'. You can also select 'People associated with a specific event type' by setting the Event Type and the maximum/minimum frequency. If you want to create a set using 'People with custom attributes', you can enter the Event Name on which this set is to be based. If your uploaded file has custom attributes, you can use those as well.

Method 2: An alternate method is to create it from the Audiences section. Navigate to Create Audience and then select 'Custom Audience' from the drop-down list. You will see a heading 'How do you want to create this audience' with several options – Custom File, Website Traffic, App Activity, Offline Activity, and Engagement. If you look at the 'Offline

113

Activity' option, you will see: 'create a list of people who interacted with your business in-store, by phone, or through other offline channels'. Select the Offline Event set and create an audience set with 'People who interacted offline..'. If you see it this way, it is similar to 'Everyone in the event set' that we had selected in the Method one above. Now select the event and you will have an option to further add filters in 'Refine by' such as Custom Data, Value or Aggregated Value. If you chose 'Value', you can add a logic for the value and frequency for 'Aggregated Value'.

Define your Target Audience

You have defined your ad objective. The next step is to define your target audience using various attributes, such as location, gender, age etc. Connect with those who love what you are doing. Billions of people use Facebook every month and with the power of the audience selection tool, Facebook can tell you who the right set of audiences are for your business. You can utilize your knowledge about your customers by looking for others who share similar interests and likes. You can use three ways to select your audience on Facebook – Core audience, Custom audience, and Lookalike audience.

- **Core Audience**: You can select who you want to target – your core audience based on location, demographics, likes, and interests etc.
- **Custom Audience**: This feature helps you get in touch with those you already know. So, reconnect with your existing contacts and customers on Facebook and build your audience base. These can be your loyal customers who did purchase from you in the past, your site visitors who visited your website, or mobile users who showed interest in your business through

the mobile app. By connecting with them, you can drive more sales.

- **Lookalike Audience**: You can build your audience based on users who are similar to your existing customers. Through Facebook, you can find people who share the similar interests or likes as your existing customers. Lookalike audiences utilize the insights gained from Facebook marketing to enhance the possibility of reaching all those who might be interested in what you do.

Setting your targeting is a key step because if you do not target the right set of people, your messaging will never reach who it should. This would result in failure as you will not get the outcome you had expected from your ads. You must think about what sort of audience you should be targeting: the age group, men or women, their location, their hobbies, their interests, their likes, and dislikes. It's obvious that you will get better results from ads that are targeted to people who are interested in what you do – here, quality matters more than quantity. So, even if you are able to reach ten people who are interested in your business, it is better than 50 random people. Because of this, Facebook always recommends reaching out to smaller but more focused groups.

Here are the attributes you should consider to find your targeting audience:

Location: This is where your potential customers live. The main field you need to enter is country and rest all is optional. If you want to target all the people in a country, do not add any other information. But if your product is specific to a state or city, then add further filters, such as 'By State/Province' and not the filter 'Everywhere'. If you are selling something locally, then you will have to specify the required fields accordingly.

Demographics: You can set the parameters such as sex, age etc. as part of demographics for your customers. If you want it to be generic, you can set the demographics as 'Any' but that's not an effective way of advertising. For example, if you are advertising a product that is meant to reach out only to females in the age group of 45-65, Facebook will show your ad to exactly the defined audience. If you do not go with the exact match filter, your ad will be shown to males and youngsters. By selecting the right demographics, you increase the effectiveness of your Facebook Ad and will receive additional discounted clicks and impressions with the defined target range.

Likes and Interests: This is one of the important parameters as you must try to be as descriptive as possible with your keywords. Facebook can help you find more options, so if you just enter the main keyword, a list of options will be shown and you can then select what's most appropriate.

Unlike some other platforms where you can enter any keywords, you have to enter only the words that Facebook has available in its database. This improves the potential of your description and ensures the words you choose are truly relevant to the specific ad. Facebook comes up with these keywords based on activities, likes, interests, favorite TV soaps, movies etc. that a specific user likes, and it collects this information from user's profile. Facebook even considers the groups, communities, and pages liked by users as these also help in understanding what he/she is interested in. For example, if you are selling wildlife-themed skirts, you might choose the keyword 'wildlife' and your ad would then be displayed to all those who love wildlife, have checked-in to wildlife places, such as jungles and forests.

In order to give you options for new related keywords, Facebook also looks into the keywords that are most popular among the users you are trying to target. When you add these keywords to your targeting, it will increase the number of people you are targeting, while still ensuring you reach out to those who are interested in what you are doing or selling. Spend some time on this parameter and see what the most relevant keywords are. Targeting the right set of people is of utmost importance.

Connections: This parameter helps you target users who are connected with you through the pages, groups, or events you are managing. You can choose to leave this parameter as 'Anyone', but if you want to be more specific about who you want it to reach, check the advanced options. Browse through the 'Show Advanced Targeting Options' and you will see that there are additional options for you to select, such as demographics, interests etc.

Birthday: You can reach out to your target audience on their birthday. Using this option, you can display very specific ads to your users on their birthday. For instance, you organize custom tailored events and reach out to your target audience giving them options on how they can celebrate their birthday. You can run the ad over a period of certain days and if someone in your target audience has a birthday in that period, they would be able to see it. So, if you are offering a birthday specific service or product, go for this filter.

Relationship: You can choose the marital status of your target customers. Facebook gives you five options – All, Married, Engaged, In a Relationship and Single. If you are not targeting any specific type of profiles, you can select 'All'. But if you are, choose one of the options based on what you are offering. For example, if you run a matrimonial site, you can select 'Single' so that your ad is shown to all those who are still not engaged or married.

Languages: If you are targeting a set of people who can speak a specific language, you can make the choice here. If you display your ads in French, select French. This is helpful because there is no point showing your ad to people in other countries where they do not understand French. So, if your target audience uses a different language to access their Facebook account, choose that language. Otherwise, or even when you are not sure, just leave this option blank.

Education: Facebook gives you four options to choose from – All, College Grad, In College and In High School. While most of the advertisers generally choose All, some even mention their choice here (if they are targeting a specific group of students). So, choose this option only when you can define your target audience on the basis of their education status.

Workplaces: You can mention the name of a company, organization or wherever your target customers work. You will see that adding this filter will decrease the numbers. If you don't want that to happen, leave it blank. It is good for those advertisers who are planning an ad campaign for a specific company.

These are some of the parameters you can set to define your target audience. Each time you make a choice, Facebook analyzed and re-calculates the size of your customer base.

Decide the Ad Placement

The most important thing is to decide the ad placement – where you want the ad to run. Ad placement plays a key role so the ads are visible to the target audience – not just on Facebook, but also on other social media platforms such as Instagram, Messenger etc. This is because not all your users use only Facebook or only, so display your ad on multiple platforms. The good news is Facebook has made it really simple for you. You can now post the ad across various channels with just a few clicks. You can have your ads placed in instant articles, feeds, right columns and so on. This way you improve your reach and grow your audience base. The primary advantage of tailoring your assets by placement is you do not need to create multiple ad sets and ads. You can just create one ad unit and assign multiple options to it.

Facebook also allows you show your ads on multiple devices. So, reach your audience on the device they use most extensively. To do all this, you do not have to build and place the ad again and again. You just build it once, and the Automatic Placements feature of Facebook will take care of the rest. Isn't amazing!

Another new place that is available for Facebook marketers is Marketplace. Consider it similar to Craigslist where users can browse through different items and services for sale with the focus being on local. In Marketplace, you can also sell your own items by simply clicking on 'Sell Something'. Marketers can also place their ads on their platform and viewers can see them on their mobile devices. You are just adding the ads in one more place, in addition to audience network, News Feed, and Instagram.

To use the placement for Marketplace, choose the marketing objective from conversions, consideration, or awareness. Next, edit the placement of the ad to set the Facebook Placement option.

Now, set the ad creative options from the available list.

Setting your Budget

Budget is a cost control tool on Facebook that helps you control the total amount you want to spend on an ad or ad campaign. You can set the budget for an ad or ad campaign. There are two types of budget – Daily Budget and Lifetime Budget.

While Daily Budget is the average amount you will spend on an ad or ad campaign per day, Lifetime Budget is the amount you are willing to spend on an ad or ad campaign for the time it runs.

The most common way of buying ads on Facebook is through the Ad Management tool, known as the Ads Manager. Create and submit the ad to the ad auction to purchase it. Ad auction is something that decides which ad will be displayed to which set of people. This is not something that Facebook decides – you are the sole authority for your ads. When you create the ads, you provide all the information regarding the display. Based on this information provided by you, the auction displays the specific ad to the people who are most likely to be interested in it, and for a price decided by you. The information that you provide at the ad creation time include parameters for budget (the total amount that you are willing to spend on your ad or ad campaign on daily basis or lifetime), Audience (people who you want to see this ad; you can use various attributes to connect to such people) and

Creatives (how you want these ads to look – in the form of text, images or videos).

Campaign Budget Optimization – Marketers who use Facebook to advertise can use this feature to set a budget at the campaign level that can be then optimized for ad sets with that campaign to get some great results. Normally, Daily or Lifetime budget is set at the ad set level. For example – let us say you have a campaign with two ad sets and you are willing to spend a total of $30 US for your campaign. You might allocate this budget equally:

Ad Set 1 → USD 15

Ad Set 2 → USD 15

The total budget is distributed between the two ad sets irrespective of how they perform. But with Campaign Budget Optimization, the total budget can be optimized to derive best results, based on how each ad set performs. Here's an example:

Without Optimization – Ad Set 1 is allotted $15 US and Ad Set 2 is allotted $15 US

With Campaign Budget Optimization – Campaign is allotted $30 US; Ad Set 1 is the highest performing ad set. So, Ad Set 1 is allotted $20 US and Ad Set 2 is allotted $10 US.

This is not split testing – Facebook analyzes the given ad sets and distributes the budget based on how each of them performs. It is a feature that benefits most marketers while they are running campaigns that comprise of multiple ad sets. This feature of optimization is available and can be used for all types of ad objectives. Once the marketer enables this feature for a campaign, he will have an option to set a daily budget for each ad set.

To activate the Campaign Budget Optimization at the campaign level, move the slider to activate the feature and optimize your budget across all the available ad sets. The next thing you are asked to set is the Campaign Bid Strategy, which is set at the ad set level. Next, set the campaign budget as Daily or Lifetime, and then enter a value. With Daily, you can spend more or less than the amount you mention as it gets averaged out for each day. But if you set Lifetime budget, you will never exceed the amount you enter.

To activate the Campaign Budget Optimization at the ad set level, you do not have to do it explicitly as you have already set it at the campaign level (and the same flows down to the ad set level). But you can add some control over how it is distributed among the ad sets by setting the 'Ad Set Spend Limits'. You can set a minimum level and Facebook will do its best to never exceed that limit, however, there are certain attributes that can hinder this process.

The Campaign Budget Optimization feature offered by Facebook works best when:

- You can set a budget at the campaign level and can have some flexibility in how it is distributed among the ad sets of the campaign
- You want to get the best results from a set campaign
- You want to simplify the campaign set up the process and save the time it takes to manage the budgets manually

Use your dollars efficiently and give your business an easy way to manage its budget using Campaign Budget Optimization.

Pricing: You can define the suggested cost for your ad campaign clicks depending on the targeting options you have selected (we discussed this in the previous section). The cost that you suggest is the maximum amount you are willing to pay for the ads. However, in most of the cases, you will pay less than this defined amount. The cost estimate provided is a dynamic value that changes each time you add or remove any parameter in the targeting option. This is because these parameters defined the competition of your business in the marketplace and by changing them, you are changing the competitiveness of your business. Therefore, it is recommended that you spend some time on the targeting option and check the impact on the pricing factor and the impact to other parameters. This way you should be able to reach a reasonable bid for your ad clicks.

Facebook offers its advertisers two different ways to set pricing.: Pay for Impressions (CPM) or Pay for Clicks (CPC).

Cost-per-Impression or CPM is the cost that an advertiser has to pay when his advertisement is shown per thousand impressions. It is an important metric to track the performance of a Facebook Ad. It gives the advertisers an idea of their return on investment (ROI) for their ad campaign. The advertiser has to bid on this cost before the ad goes live. CPM is an ideal strategy for the advertisers whose marketing objective is brand awareness as the cost is calculated for every 1000 impressions regardless of whether someone clicked on it or not.

Cost-per-Click or CPC is the cost that an advertiser pays when someone clicks on his ad. This strategy is most effective for those who have Call-to-action Ad Campaigns, where the customers are persuaded to take an action or make purchases. They show their interest by clicking on your Facebook Ad. Always remember that whatever the amount your bid is, you will never pay more than that as that is the maximum limit set for your ad. Facebook doesn't guarantee its users any number of clicks or impressions, so the higher the bid you place, the more probable it is to be shown to your target audience.

Bid Strategies

Advertisers are always looking for ways to fight instability related to cost and scale. There are advertising bid strategies that can improve these attributes. If you are not seeing the cost per event that you want or if you are struggling to maintain cost stability while raising your advertising budget, bid strategies can help.

Your ads are distributed based on the auction format. The cost to reach a particular user will depend on this bid, as well as various other attributes. Although Facebook does offer you the automatic bidding option, if advertisers want to control their costs, they can choose manual bidding as the underlying goal of manual bidding is to achieve the required cost per action (where action can be anything including conversions). To be able to achieve more stable and lower costs, there are two bid strategy options that are available to users – Lower Cost and Target Cost.

- **Lower Cost Bid Strategy**: Also known as automatic bidding, Facebook came up with the concept of the Lower Cost Bid Strategy to achieve lower cost per event considering the total budget. The benefit of this strategy is the efficiency it offers its users. You get the lowest cost per event. However, the main downside of choosing the Lower Cost Bid Strategy is that the low cost that you see is only a designated time. The results might be different when the competition increases or you spend more.

For the Lower Cost Bid Strategy, the most important thing is setting bid cost. Facebook allows you to set a bid cap if you wish to control the amount to be spent. If the budget is set too low, Facebook might struggle to spend it for the event. However, it can protect you from crossing your budget/spend. For instance – if a conversion is worth $5, it prevents you from spending a cost per conversion of $5.50 or more. You can set the bid cap accordingly knowing that's the maximum amount you will spend on your event.

Setting a bid cap is quite simple. You can start with the average amount you spent on prior campaigns. This is recommended to learn from previous experiences. Evaluate and decide on the most you can spend on an event so that you can see profits. Once you decide on the bid cap, Facebook recommends you have a daily budget that is at least five times more than this bid cap amount. This is because at least 50 events should be done in a week to optimize the ads. All this is part of a learning phase. Once you know what is right for your campaign, you can even increase the bid cap if you feel that you are not seeing the returns that you are expecting. The bid cap depends on the results you are seeing from your campaigns. Facebook can only make a recommendation. Only you know what's best for you. Facebook doesn't know what value the event is going to bring to your business. If you feel you are overspending with Facebook's recommendation, do not allow that to happen. Tweak it the way you want. On the other hand, you might want to set a higher bid cap value to see better distribution.

- **Target Cost Bid Strategy**: Also known as manual bidding, the Target Cost Bid Strategy is helpful if your ad objectives include conversions, catalog sales, lead generation, and app installs. This strategy should be used to achieve more stable results as you increase your spending on your campaign. As part of this strategy, you need to set a target cost depending on what have you selected as your conversion window – 1-day view or 7-day click etc. Setting the right target cost is important and, to start with, you can use an average amount on a cost per event basis. Lower this amount as much as you can till you find the lowest amount you can use to spend your entire budget. The best thing about using this strategy is that you have a stable cost per event, which is particularly helpful when you are scaling. One downside of the Target Cost Bid Strategy is higher cost fluctuations until you complete the learning phase. Once you set the target cost, Facebook will always try to get the cost per event close to this value even though you might find that the costs have been much lower. Hence, the target cost should be used cautiously.

Keeping all these things in mind, you need to decide the target cost. There is no one answer to this question as the value changes from case to case. In most cases, you should choose the default value of lowest cost without a cap, but having a bid cap on the upper limit so that Facebook doesn't spend more than what you want. Generally, the Target Cost Bid Strategy should be used when you plan to scale or increase your budget or wish to run the campaign for the long-term. This is because using this strategy would result in a more stable cost per event.

Select an Appropriate Format for your Ad Story

Facebook offers you some of the most effective and amazing options for your ad story. Whether you want it to be a combination of text and images, videos, or just images – Facebook has an ad format for every kind of story. Based on your business objective and audience, and how you want it to look on the devices, decide the format that works the best for your business.

Photo Ads: Use impactful images to make your ads attractive and visually effective. You can use Facebook's east option to make photo ads. So, if 'images' is your chosen format based on your business objectives and target audience, increase your business awareness and reach out to each one of those people who might be interested in these beautiful images. Photo ads are one of the most effective ways to attract the attention of people.

Video Ads: Video Ads have the power to move people and shake them up. Facebook knows this space very well and they have designed their advertising options on Instagram, Audience Network, and Facebook. Generally, people like to watch the short videos on-the-go (making them perfect for mobile devices) while the longer videos are something they like watching in the comfort of their home. Get on their network by capturing attention using short bursts of information, introducing new products and increasing brand awareness. When you want to share complex messages, use mid-roll video ads to tell your longer stories. As these are non-skippable ads, they are meant to be as disruptive as possible. If you want to reach people beyond this platform, Facebook has an option to expand its in-stream ads to various other sites as well. For this, use mid-roll and pre-roll ads. In-stream videos are something that helps you reach out to your connections when they are in a relaxed watching mode. They are also termed as "capture attention" videos as these ads capture the attention of viewers for longer times. About 70-75% of the ad impressions are mostly played with the sound on and to completion. As these in-stream ads cannot be skipped, they can be used to share more complex messages. Not everybody can anybody publish these ads. Facebook allows only select users create and publish these in-stream ads if they qualify the defined eligibility criteria for these ads. These ads won't appear until at least 60 secs into the video, so the person viewing the video would be totally engaged in watching when the ad appears.

These video ads can:

- The Facebook Video ads compliment your sales that happen on other channels, e.g. TV. There are certain sets of people, especially young people, who are difficult to reach on other channels, such as radio and television. Facebook Video ads help you reach them.
- It spreads the message in an innovate world. In today's digital world where everything is happening

creatively, even the messages should be spread innovatively, and these emerging videos help you achieve that.

Carousel Ads: You can show multiple videos or images in a single ad. With this format, you can showcase up to ten videos or images in a single advertisement, but each of these ads will have its own separate link. Using this format, you can showcase multiple products or multiple features of a single product or service. You can even tell a story to your audience with the help of these carousel ads. This format is much effective than other formats because carousels are more interactive, more flexible, and have much more interactive space to tell your brand or product story.

Slideshow Ads: Using slideshows can connect with your customers by creating cost-effective video ads from available videos and/or images. Slideshow ads are not video ads; they are video-like ads that comprise of text, sound, and visuals to tell a story, hence tapping into the power of videos. Creating these slideshow ads from available still images and videos is very simple and very effective. Some of the reasons why you might want to use these ads are:

- Slideshows have a captivating format that can effectively capture the attention of the viewer.
- They are very easy to create; they can even be created on-the-go on mobile devices.
- Slideshow ads work everywhere – even in places with a bad connection or poor speed where reaching people is a challenge.

Collection Ads: Collection Ads showcase multiple products with their features in a single ad. With a collection ad, you can browse multiple products or get detailed information about the features of a product. Collection Ads are highly valuable in today's digital world where people are spending more and more time on their devices to discover and learn about the new products and their features. These ads are a seamless and interactive experience, which makes it easier for users to browse through the products and purchase the ones that interest them.

To be able to create a collection, you have to create a product catalog that includes a dynamic or static feed of products you plan to sell. A product catalog can be created by logging into the Business Manager and selecting Product Catalogs from the Settings tab. Click on 'Add New Product Catalogs' and then create a new catalog. You will be asked to give your catalog a name and then select a type (Products, Hotels, Flights). Once done, click on 'Create Product Catalog'. Next, you can add people who can access this product catalog; this is not a mandatory step, so you can skip it if you want. Then select the pixels that will lead the user to the page where the selected product from the catalog can be bought. You can skip this step if you have uploaded the static file, but if you are trying to run a dynamic ad, add the information required. Now click on 'Add Product Feed' and the name it. Now upload the product feed file – it could be in csv, tsv, or any other format.

Messenger Ads: This is a new way of connecting with new and existing customers by using the power of Facebook's target messaging. Since quite a lot of people interact with the businesses through Messenger, these Messenger Ads are an effective way to reach them. The easiest and most effective way to reap benefits of this format is to run ads on the Home page of the messenger application. Messenger ads are no different than other ad formats available on Facebook – the way you interact with each format is different. This way you can also touch base with the customers you haven't interacted with for a while.

Let the Games Begin: Creating Ads

Ads on Facebook can be created by:

- Using Business Manager
- Using Ads Manager
- Catalog Ads
- Ads Manager App
- Creative Hub

Business Manager

Business Manager is a Facebook tool created to manage pages and accounts on Facebook. With this tool, you can manage your access to pages, add accounts on Facebook, and work with agencies so that they can manage to advertise on your behalf. With your Business Manager account, you can have multiple users and accounts combined. It is designed to add a layer of organization, management, and security to the management features available by default.

Business Manager is just like the page manager on steroids, as not many people know about it. The most compelling reasons to use it is *focus*. While using other page management tools, you might feel that you are just using the basic features of your personal account, but that's not the case with Business Manager. It offers its users an appropriated interface with all the assets needed for your business, and without any personal elements.

Another reason to use Business Manager is *organization*. We all like things to be structured, just the way our ads are. We have ad sets within the Ad Campaigns, and these ad sets have ads. Business Manager also structures your pages in a similar fashion. At the top level, you have your brand, within that, you have your Pages, and within each of these Facebook Pages, you have all your assets. If you are using these pages for multiple customers, you can add them all under this Business Manager so that you have all the details in one place. This also gives you a clear view of all your business assets – you have your pages, your team as well as your ads, everything in one place.

There are two roles available in Business Manager to manage your ads on Facebook – admin and employee. Here's an overview of each of these roles (ref: Facebook.com)

	Admin	**Employee**
Add and remove employees and partners	Can	Cannot
View settings for the business	Can	Can
Change business settings	Can	Cannot
Add pages, ad accounts or other assets	Can	Cannot
Be assigned to Pages, ad accounts or other assets	Can	Can

To be able to publish an ad on Facebook, you must have a Business Manager account that manages at least one Facebook Page or more. You can do this by following these steps:

1. Browse through the Business Manager settings page
2. Select pages from the People and Assets tab
3. Add a new page by clicking on Add a New Page
4. Select one of the options from – Claim a Page, Request Access to a Page, or Create a New Page
5. Fill in the required details

The three options available are: Claiming an existing page, Requesting Access to an existing page, or Creating a New page.

Claiming an existing Page: Say you have one or two business pages, a couple of ads and some business assets. When you click on *Claim Assets* in the left column, you will be taken to another list of options that are the types of assets – ad account, page, or an app. Click one that fits your requirement and you will go to a Claim Wizard where you will add your apps, business pages, ad accounts, and various other assets. You cannot claim assets and pages you do not own because if you claim someone else's page, the actual owner of that asset will not be able to claim it. If by mistake you claim the assets, some of them cannot be removed once added. Double check the assets you claim. However, if you are simply managing an asset for someone else, get the actual owner to set up Business Manager, and then you can request access using your account. Additionally, you can add your Instagram account to your Business Manager. Just browse through the Settings and click on Claim An Instagram Account.

If you want to add an account to Business Manager, follow these steps:

1. Browse through the Business Manager settings page
2. Select Ad Accounts from the People and Assets tab
3. Add a new account by clicking on Add New Ad Accounts
4. Select one of the options: Claim Ad Account, Request Access to an Ad Account, or Create a New Ad Account
5. Fill in the required details

Once you have added the required account, you need to set it up by filling in the required information, such as company's address, name, setting up the billing and payment information, and reviewing your notification settings.

Requesting access to an existing asset: If you are working with other pages or ad accounts that you do not own, they cannot be added to your Business Manager. What you can do is request access to those pages so that you can edit them. The first step in this process is to have Business Manager set up for the person who owns the ad account. You can either set it up for them or ask them to set up themselves. Once it is done, use your account to find the page and add the asset/assets you will be managing for them. The request will go to them for approval and once approved, you should be able to manage their assets.

Creating a New Business Assets: If you want another (secondary) page for your business or are looking to have a franchise page, or you need another ad account on Facebook, you can do so using the 'create New business assets' option. When you click on 'Add New' from the 'Claim Assets' tab, it will see different types of assets, such as ad accounts, pages, payment methods, people, and product catalogs that you can add to your Business Manager. Once selected, you will be taken to a Wizard to complete the process by filling in the required details.

Ads Manager

Facebook has two tools for advertising management purposes – Facebook Ads Manager and Power Editor. Both are free tools, but if you are a newbie in the world of Facebook advertising, using Facebook Ads Manager is recommended as Power Editor is a little complex.

Using Facebook Ads Manager, you can:

- Create new ads and ad sets
- Create new Ad Campaigns
- Manage ad bids
- Target various kinds of audience
- Optimize your campaigns
- Track the performance of your campaigns
- A/B test your Ad Campaigns

To be able to set up and use Ads Manager, you need to understand Ad Campaigns. Ad Campaigns will be explained later in this ebook, but the following is an overview of what Ad Campaigns are.

For any advertisement to run on Facebook, it requires three elements – a campaign, an ad set and an ad. These elements combine together to form something known as a campaign structure by which you can run ads on Facebook the way you want and reach the right set of people more effectively.

When the advertising objective is set, it is at the **campaign level**. This is where you decide what you want to achieve through your ads – get more likes, generate more sales, or increase brand awareness. The targeting strategy is defined at the **ad set** level by setting up various parameters, such as budget, target, placement etc. The **ads** are actually the creatives, such as images, videos etc. that attract an audience to know about your business.

In simple words, an ad campaign is the foundation of the ad and, therefore, when you want to create an ad, you will start with creating the ad campaign. You decide your advertising goal and then start by creating the ad set.

The ad set is what tells you what to run as part of the ad. Select the audience for your ad set using the targeting option available. A campaign can have several ad sets, each will have different budgeting, targeting, and scheduling.

Lastly, the ad – this is what your audience will see. The ads are created within an ad set by including various elements, such as images, text, videos etc. An ad set can have multiple ads within it.

Effective Facebook Ad Campaigns

To set up a campaign on Facebook, browse through the top left menu and select the Ads Manager tool. Go to the top right side and click on Create Ad. You will now be taken through the process.

The main focus to create an ad campaign should be to reach your target audience. One of the reasons the campaign doesn't perform well is that it doesn't reach the people you intended to reach. Those who are interested are not targeted, and those who are targeted never bother to look at the campaigns. Implications – You will see a dip in engagement levels, there will be an increase in a number of negative reviews as the right audience is not targeted, CPM will go up and eventually the campaign will no longer be effective and profitable. In an ideal scenario, elements that make a campaign effective are:

- The targeted audience add value
- The targeted audience maintain quality
- The promotions add value

All these things should be essentially there in a campaign to make it effective and evergreen. Here is what needs to be done:

1. **Define the Funnel**: Before you get into the nitty-gritty of campaigns and ads, define the basic funnel that you would be working with. For this, you must set your Campaign Trigger and Campaign Goal. And note these two values should be related. You cannot have a campaign trigger that is associated with a goal, which is not even related to it. if you have an effective Campaign trigger, you would achieve your Campaign Goal. For example, you have a free demo session about English learning as the trigger and sign-ups for a related English learning program as the campaign goal.

2. **Define the Trigger**: Now that you have defined the basic tunnel for your advertising on Facebook, it is time to think about the people who will help you perform the trigger. Some of the good examples of campaign triggers are – registering for something,

purchasing a product related to the actual goal, engaging with specific posts or videos.

3. **Create Audience for the defined trigger**: You know your funnel and you have defined the trigger. Next – define your target audience who would perform this trigger during the course of time. The kind of audience you can target for some of the triggers:

   a. If your trigger is purchasing a product which is related to the actual goal, you can create Custom Audience using your website. For example – you can see who all hit the thank you page after buying a product from your website.

   b. If your trigger is registering for something, you can create Custom Audience by checking who all registered for something on your website in last few days. You can also use Lead Ads to know who registered via the given method in last few days.

   c. If your trigger is engaging with a specific post or video, you can create a Custom Audience by analyzing who watched your video or read your post in last few days. But in this case, you should be careful about those who read your posts or watched your video multiple times.

Create Campaign

- Select objective

Create Ad Set

- Set Audience
- Select Placement

- Set Budget and Schedule

Create Ad

- Select the Format
- Choose Media
- Select Additional Creative

If you understand this structure, it will be very easy to set up an ad campaign on Facebook.

Step 1: As it can be seen from the flow diagram, to create an ad campaign, you first need to select the objective of your advertising. You can choose from one of the following options:

- Brand awareness
- Local awareness
- Reach
- Traffic
- Engagement
- All installs
- Video views
- Lead generation
- Conversions
- Product catalog sales
- Store visits

Choose the objective based on what you are trying to achieve through your ad. This is the key as various other attributes are determined based on your ad goals – bidding, ad format etc. Once Facebook knows your goals, it will do its best to drive the best results to help you achieve them.

Step 2: Tag your Ad Campaign with an appropriate and catchy name.

This is quite self-explanatory. However, whatever name you think of, make sure it is in line with your ad objective and comes with the date stamp for easy navigation.

Step 3: Select your target audience

To select your target audience, you are given two choices by Facebook – you either create a new set of your target audience or use a saved one. Some people try to create Custom Audience at this stage, however, an important thing to note here is that you cannot create Custom Audience at this level, but you can use Custom Audience that you had created previously in the Audience Manager. So, select your target audience to proceed further.

Step 4: Decide where you want to place your Facebook ads

You have an option to place your Facebook ads on any of these platforms – Instagram, Facebook News Feed, Facebook Right pane, In-stream videos, Audience Network and Instant Articles. Apart from these options, you can also select Automatic Placement, allowing Facebook to decide the best placement for your ads. Experts recommend the following ad placements:

- If you want to increase brand awareness, you should post your ads on Facebook and Instagram.
- If your advertising goal is Engagement, you should post your ads on Facebook and Instagram.
- If your objective is Video Views, you should post your ads on Facebook, Audience Network, and Instagram.
- If you want to increase the traffic, you should post your ads on Facebook and Audience Network.

- To increase the number of conversions, you should post on Facebook and Audience Network.
- If the advertising goal is Ad Installs, you should post the ads on Facebook, Audience Network, and Instagram.

Step 5: The next step involves setting up a budget and bids for the ad campaign on Facebook

Step 6: Select the ad type and insert images or video. To create an ad, you can either use an existing post or create a new ad.

Lead Generation with Facebook Ads

You want to generate more leads from these Facebook ads and create ads on Facebook to promote your lead magnet.

With its exceptional targeting capabilities, Facebook ads offer a brilliant way to reach out all those who are interested in your offerings. You need to set up a system using these ads that help generate leads.

1) **Know your customers** – Facebook is massive and loaded with information, and you just get few seconds to win the attention of your audience. If you cannot make use of this opportunity, you lose the game. You need to focus on how to craft a catchy message that catches the attention of your potential customers. You don't want them to scroll past your posts. This can be only achieved when you know your customers well when you know what they are looking for, what sort of problems they are facing, what questions they have, what is it that they don't like and so on. You can

get all this information from online forums, their profiles, their comments, and the conversations you have with them in various groups and communities. The more information you get from your customers, the more effective your ads will be.

2) **Offer them a freebie** – Giving something valuable to your customers is always an effective way to gain their attention. This is known as a "lead magnet". Remember that your offering shouldn't sound 'salesy'. Offer them something that helps them solve their problem or achieve something they have been longing for. This way they will see you as someone who can add value to their goals, and will build trust. These freebies should also be designed to create a great impression of your business or brand. If you don't know what to offer, get help from your audience. Ask them to complete a questionnaire or take a survey that will help you know what they want to achieve. This way, you will also know their likes and dislikes. All this can help you think of a lead magnet.

3) **Include a Thank you page** – Once you have decided what to offer your customers as a giveaway, you should find out who you can give it to. Here is another opportunity for driving traffic. You can host your freebie on a page and encourage people to click the link/fill the form/reply to the questions/give their email address to receive the freebie. The web page you will use to achieve this is known as a "squeeze page" as it squeezes the audience to take an action either by providing the details or leaving the page. To build this kind of pages, there are several tools

available on the market these days, such as Instapage, Leadpages etc. You should mention the benefits of your freebie so that your audience is motivated to opt-in. Also, it is recommended to include a privacy statement that says you will keep their data safe and secured. It is also good to create a thank you page for all those who chose to opt-in.

4) **Track actions using Pixel** – Facebook offers a code that once placed in the website helps you easily track activities on your page and links them back to your advertising account on Facebook. If you want to do this, browse through the Pixels that appear as one of the Assets in Ad Manager. Within Pixels, click on Actions and then click on 'View Pixel Code'. This will show you your Pixel code that is unique to each ad account. Copy this Pixel code from that page by clicking on the box. This needs to be added to the thank you page linked to the squeeze page so that you can track the activities and optimize your ads on Facebook. Navigate to the thank you page and paste this copied code between the header tags. If the code is being added to the Lead pages, then click on Lead Page options. Now click on the Tracking Codes and add the code in the space available. By adding this code to the thank you page, you are telling the platform that all the people who view your ad should click on your squeeze page and provide the details before they are navigated to the thank you page. However, it is important to note that if you are trying to build Custom Audience for retargeting, then this code must be included on the squeeze page and all other web pages.

5) **Know who should see your ad** – Use Ad Targeting Options. Before you create your ad, you must know who it should target (who should see it). The goal while choosing your target audience is to define your audience in a very distinctive manner. Some of the filters that can help you do this are Demographics, Interests, and Behaviors. Three major categories are provided so that you can use the one you have information about. For instance – if you don't know the behavior and interests of your target audience, you can use demographics targeting to determine who should see your ads. This means when you focus on specific demographics, you will get better results as you are targeting the people who should be interested in your ad, as per your analysis.

Next, know what content the target audience might be interested in: consider what events they attend, what type of content they have been reading, what pages they follow, which newspaper they subscribe to, which movies they watch and so on. Once you find out some of the pages they like and follow, add them in the sidebar. If you are aware of their interests and/or behavior, click on Advanced and add. Facebook will then generate an updated list of pages that they might like based on their interests and behavior. Similarly, you can also exclude certain groups that you feel your target audience wouldn't like.

6) **Create Ads that interest your target audience** – Now that you have defined your target audience, you can create ads that might appeal to this audience. Log into your Ads Manager and create a new ad by

clicking on 'Create New Ad' and then 'Creating New Campaign'. Select the ad objective as 'Increase Conversion on your website' as you are looking to optimize and track the actions on your site. Name your campaign. Once this is done, assign the custom conversion to the ad set by giving it an appropriate name. Change the ad set settings and select a placement. You also need to select a budget – daily budget works fine in this case. Have a start and end date for it.

Create an ad for this ad set by including all the details that will get your message across to your target audience. Check for phrases and words that Facebook doesn't allow and ensure you do not include them in your ad. Focus on the copy that helps your audience solve their issues or helps them achieve what they want to achieve. Once you are done, submit the ad for review and you will see your new campaign has been set, along with the ad set and the ad created.

If you want to run the same ad for another audience, you can do so simply by duplicating the ad set and editing the target audience for this duplicated copy. To create a duplicate copy, click on 'Create Similar Ad Set' and then click on Edit to change the targeting settings. Give a new name to the new ad set and click on Save to create it. This way you can create as many copies as you want to serve different types of audiences.

7) **Analyze your ads** – Once you run your ads for a couple of days, gather enough data that can be analyzed to derive important results. You can see

these results in Ads Manager and this data is based on the ad objective you have used to create the ad. The table for conversion for the ads you have created displays the number of conversions you achieved from the ads displayed to the audience and the amount it cost to achieve the conversion for various types of audiences.

There are other things that you can analyze and track. To see the details, click on Columns on top of the table and select Customize Columns. You can select the data you want to include in the table so that you can compare and track and order it to suit your requirements. Select all the data you want to be included and click on Apply. Here are some of the things you might want to track – Click-through rate (CTR) to know the interest of your audience toward your ad, Number of website conversions achieved, Number of website clicks you received, Frequency with which each person from your target set has seen your ad. You can select the attributes and save it as a template so that you can use it in the future by checking the box that states 'Save as Preset' and name this template so that it's easy to use again.

Once you have a system that can effectively and efficiently generate a lead for your ads, you can set it up and run in the autopilot mode. This will help you enhance your customer relationship and engage with them better.

Conversion Optimization by Facebook

You have an item that you want to advertise on Facebook, and you have also created an ad campaign, now decide if your ad objective is conversion or traffic. Facebook gives you an option to optimize your ads for both – Conversion and Clicks. Facebook ads can be optimized for your specific ad objective. Facebook is loaded with data and it knows which set of people are more likely to convert, click, or engage. To utilize this intelligence, Facebook gives you an option to select an action that you wish to optimize –

- Conversions: Make your ads reach the right set of people so that you can get more website conversions for a low cost.
- Clicks: Make your ads reach the right set of people so that you can get more clicks from your ad to the required destination (which could be a link on or off Facebook) for a low cost.
- Impressions: Make your ads reach people as many times as possible.
- Daily Unique Reach: Make your ads reach people at least once in a day.

The power of advertising can be realized from Conversion and Clicks. And when you chose to optimize your ads by one of these actions, Facebook will not show your ads to everyone in your audience set. Rather, it will focus only on those who it thinks are likely to perform the required action (clicks or conversion).

Clicks or Conversion

If you want to drive more sales, it makes sense to optimize for conversions. Once you have decided your action, you need to tell Facebook which conversion, and in particular, you want to optimize. For instance, if you are trying to sell your English learning course, you want to optimize your ads for that. If you have installed Facebook Pixel and also created a custom conversion for the course, Facebook would know what sort of people have bought this course before and who is likely to buy (based on historical data). A problem occurs when there is no historical data – if the product is new and no one has bought it in the past. Facebook will not have historical data to analyze future results for the product. According to Facebook experts, to optimize systems effectively, it should get at least 15-25 conversions per week. The more quality data, the better the results derived from Facebook. So, what should be done in cases where there are no conversions because the product is new or no conversions because an existing product isn't doing well. In such cases, you might have to optimize for a broader conversion. For instance – you can choose to optimize your ads for a general event like 'Purchase'. Another option available is to optimize link clicks to drive more traffic to your landing page in a way that it brings in more conversions. What most of the advertisers chose to do in this situation is to optimize click links and once they start seeing enough conversions, they switch to optimize that.

Click to Conversion Optimization – The switch from click to conversion optimization used to be done manually and not very effective because one should know how long to optimize for clicks before making the switch to conversions. Then Facebook introduced a new feature to automatically switch from click links to conversions. For this method, Facebook says, "If not enough people have seen your ads and taken action, we may not be able to optimize your conversions. We will optimize for link clicks until we have more data, then start optimizing for conversions." So, if you toggle the switch to turn on this feature, you will be given two options in the drop-down menu   - Standard and Extended. Standard Optimization is the default that Facebook starts optimizing for link clinks until any of the following is achieved:

- 1000 link clicks
- 15-20 conversions
- 7 days have passed

If anyone of these is achieved, Facebook automatically switches to conversions. They don't care if you have exhausted all your campaign budget or if the campaign ran for less than a week; if you have hit any of these thresholds, the switch will occur automatically.

In the case of extended optimization, Facebook optimizes for both conversions and link clicks until you start having 15 – 20 conversions or if the set budget is exhausted. If either of these thresholds is achieved, Facebook automatically switches to conversions. However, a downside of this method is although you might get more conversions, you are risking losing a lot of traffic that comes without conversion (since Facebook cannot effectively optimize all those conversions). That's why Standard is the recommended option as that's how most of the marketers found a solution to their volume problem.

Improving Facebook Ad Performance

If you are looking to increase your leads and improve the success of your business, use Facebook advertising wisely.

You can improve the performance of these ads by using the right ad set structure and creating the right audiences.

To improve the performance of Facebook ads:

- **Look for more audiences** for the existing ad campaign. If you see that your existing Facebook Ad campaigns are not giving you the required output in terms of sales, it might be because there are not enough people interested to drive sales. In such a situation, you add more audiences by uploading the existing client list and using Audience Insights to define similar clients. Once you find these similar client profiles, you can add them to your audiences.

  Upload your existing client list to Facebook – Navigate to your Facebook Ads account and click on Tools. From the drop-down menu, choose Audiences. Next, click on Create Audience and then select Custom Audience from the available menu. You will see a window for you to select how you want to create this Custom Audience. Select Customer List if you are going to upload the existing database file. Once you select Customer List, it will ask you to choose one of the given options to upload your Customer List to Facebook. You can either select Upload a file if you have an excel spreadsheet with the email address and contact details of your customers, or you can select Copy and Paste Your Custom List if you have fewer data. The last option given is to Import from MailChimp if you have an account on MailChimp so you can import your customer data using a third-party application.

Define the new client profile using Audience Insights – Using Audience Insights, you can define your new client profiles. So, click on Tools and select Audience Insights from your Facebook Ads Manager. From the options provided, click on A Custom Audience and then select the Custom Audience data you uploaded in the last step. It is always recommended to have more data as more data means better results. Once the file is uploaded, learn about different attributes of your audience. Once you click on Demographics, it will show you how your customers are distributed in terms of gender and age. You can also learn about the lifestyle of your Custom Audience including education level data, relationship status, job titles, Facebook pages liked, home ownership and so on.

- **Restructure your ad sets** to improve the performance of your ads. Some users include audiences and devices in the same ad set. This can create an issue when you wish to scale up your ad campaign due to the following reasons:
    - ✓ Having different unrelated attributes in the same ad set will not help you understand which audiences are effective and which are not.
    - ✓ Since the results are always shown at the ad set level, you will not be able to distinguish them based on target audience.
    - ✓ If you are targeting ad placements and multiple devices in the same ad set, you can segregate the results for each of these but will not be able to have specific budgets and bids for them. This means you will not be able to customize your

ads by device and target audience if they are all in one ad set.

✓ Ads that can be customized for your audience are more capable of converting and getting per results in terms of a number of clicks with the least spent.

✓ Ads that are shown on desktops are different from what is shown on mobiles. This is because the audiences that view the ads on mobiles have different needs than those who see in on their desktops.

If you want to gain control over your bids, budgets and the way audiences are targeted, it is always recommended that you separate these and have just one target audience for one ad set. Here's an example.

If your ad campaign currently looks like this:

Ad Set 1:
- o Placements – Desktop News Feed, Mobile News Feed
- o Audiences – People who are interested in Lily, Roses, Marigold; Behavior – flower growers, people buying different types of plants to grow flowers, people who shop online.

For better targeting, revise the campaign structure:

New Ad Set 1:

- o Placements – Desktop News Feed
- o Audiences – People interested in Lily, Rose, Marigold

New Ad Set 2:

- o Placements – Mobile News Feed
- o Audiences – People interested in Lily, Rose, Marigold

New Ad Set 3:

- o Placements – Desktop News Feed
- o Behavior – flower growers

New Ad Set 4:

- o Placements – Mobile News Feed
- o Behavior – flower growers

New Ad Set 5:

- o Placements – Desktop News Feed
- o Behavior – people buying different types of plants to grow flowers

New Ad Set 6:

- o Placements – Mobile News Feed
- o Behavior – people buying different types of plants to grow flowers

New Ad Set 7:

- o Placements – Desktop News Feed
- o Behavior – People who shop online

New Ad Set 8:

- o Placements – Mobile News Feed
- o Behavior – People who shop online

By using simple ways, you can improve your Facebook ads and know more about your customers. You can structure your ad sets to gain more control over budgeting and bidding. To optimize them further, you can consider doing a split test (discussed later in this book) as there can be several profiles within a smaller budget. Evaluate and see what works – change the budget for what works, and repeat this process till you find a new set of audiences based on the data you have.

Facebook Messenger Ads

There are three primary features that the messenger ads have – Messenger Destination, Messenger Home Placement, and Sponsored Messages Placement.

Messenger Destination: This permits advertisers to make ads that encourage people to have a conversation with the messenger. It is important to understand that destination is not a placement. While creating this ad, you will be given an option to choose your destination – the place where people will be directed when they click on the ad. This messenger destination will be an external URL in typical cases, but if your ad objective is to generate traffic or conversion, the messenger destination could be the Messenger also. If you decide to choose Message as your destination, you are required to upload an image for the ad you are trying to create. Once you do this, you will be asked to fill in rest of the details which include a headline, newsfeed link description etc. once all this is done, the ad looks like any other desktop News Feed item. When someone clicks on this ad, they will be redirected to a conversation within the messenger. So, you can set up what it will look like. To create an ad, click on 'Set

Up Messenger Content' and a window will pop up. The messenger content can be either text-only, or combination of text and visuals, but for now, we'll focus on text. Facebook gives you two options for doing this – Quick Creation and JSON Creation. As the name suggests, you create the ads quickly using Quick Creation, whereas JSON Creation is an advanced method that needs its own blog post. If we do it using the Quick Creation method, you will be asked to provide Introduction text, Message text as well as Buttons.

The introduction text is something that appears on top of the message text. The button is a simple link that appears below the message text and takes the user to another destination. When the user clicks on this messenger ad, he will be taken to the Facebook Messenger where he will see a welcome message. You can have multiple buttons if you want to redirect the user to different places based on what they want.

if you are including a video in your ad, you will be asked to fill in the introductory text, a video file, and quick reply option that would immediately send a message as soon as it is clicked.

Remember these destination ads –

- Are available in the News Feed – both mobile and desktop
- Are available to advertisers running campaigns with the ad objective of "page post engagement" or "Send people to a destination on or off Facebook"
- Can be used to target anyone

Some of the ways to use this type are –

1. Retargeting your audience: the biggest hindrance for an advertiser in the marketing journey is to drive

conversions. There are many users who visit your page but do not convert. So, the goal is to retarget such users with the help of these destination ads that give an extra touch point to your brand. Retarget them and see what issues they are facing. Help them with these issues so that they can build faith in your brand. Understand that people who visit your site and leave without buying, have an underlying reason for this behavior. Find out what it is by giving them a platform to ask questions and solve problems. You will see that most of them will change their attitude toward your business if you are able to solve their problem.

2. Generate awareness for cold traffic: People who have never heard of your brand are categorized as cold traffic. Using the destination ads, you can target cold traffic so that they are aware of what you do and offer. If done correctly, this will help you acquire new customers. They key is to ensure the destination ad triggers an ideal conversation.

Messenger Home Destination: The ad can appear in several different placements including mobile News Feed, desktop News Feed etc., but all these ads will ultimately direct the user to a conversation in the Facebook Messenger. Within Messenger, there are again placements available. The ad that you created can appear in two places within messenger – Home and Sponsored Messages. If you select Home, it would appear on the home screen of the user's messenger, and if you select Sponsored Messages, it would appear in a different place (details mentioned in the next category).

Sponsored Messages Placement: The ad will not only appear on the home screen but it will also appear in people's messages in Messenger. However, Facebook has a limit - you can send the message only to those who have messaged you on your page before. Also, if you choose Sponsored Messages Placement, all other placements will not work. While setting up the ad, you will also be asked to include your Facebook Page – this is important, so do not forget to include it.

Next – you need to set up your audience. The moment you click on the 'Custom Audiences', a message will appear on your screen that says 'Messenger can only be used for people who have messaged your Page. If you want to keep the Messenger Placement, choose a different audience.' This means you can only target those who have messaged your page before, and you can create this kind of audience within Page Engagement Custom Audiences.

If you have created this set before, select 'Create New' and then select 'Custom Audience'. From the options given, click on 'Engagement' and then 'Facebook Page'. You will be asked to select your Facebook Page in 'Page' and select 'People who sent a message to your Page' in 'Include'. You can set 'In the past' as 365 days so that you include a larger audience. Click on 'Create Audience' to create this audience set. You can choose targeting options as age, locations, languages and so on. All this is being done to create a target audience who have messaged your page before. So, the more filters you add, the smaller the audience.

Next, you need to set optimization for your ad delivery, and if you see you have just one option – Impressions. This will optimize your ads to be delivered to the audience as many times as possible. In order to bid, you will have to select

Manual Bid. You can enter a value here and experiment to see what works best for you.

Regarding Format, you will see that only Single Image can be selected. Also provide Headline, Call-to-action, Website URL, Link Description to create the ad. Once the ad is created, it will appear in the message box, and when clicked, it will show the image and other elements of the ad.

Things that you can do with these sponsored messages are:

- You can target only those who have messaged your page before
- You will be charged based on impressions whether the user opened the message or not
- It will be available to only the campaigns that are created with the objective of website conversions or 'send people to a destination on or off Facebook'

Creating Canvas Custom Audiences

Another great way for advertisers to create immersive experiences for users so they do not have to leave Facebook is to use Facebook Canvas. Canvas is a combination of links, text, Call-to-action buttons, videos, carousels, and product feeds that advertisers use to reach their target audience. The main advantage of using Canvas is users never have to leave Facebook and by staying on, they are presented with different kinds of media instantaneously. However, by staying on the platform, the initial click to the website landing page is not available for remarketing purposes. To fill this gap, Facebook created Canvas Custom Audience, which is another addition to engagement on Facebook. Next, you need to make a canvas and then learn how to create a Canvas Custom Audience.

Creating a new Canvas

A Facebook Canvas can be created with templates that are already available. These templates simplify and streamline the building process. Before you start creating a canvas, think about what kind of experience you want to offer to your audience, how can you engage your audience using the canvas, see if you can use the canvas templates, and have the creatives ready that you want to use for the canvas.

To create a canvas navigate to the Ads Manager. Click on Create Ad and then select an ad objective that tells why you want to create this canvas – to generate traffic, to create conversions etc. Select an objective.

Next – give a name to the campaign and then click on Continue. Once this is done, choose your placements, audience, and budget. Click Continue.

You need to pick an ad format so that it determines the type of template you want to use to create the canvas. Remember that if you select the collection format, the fullscreen Canvas will automatically be selected (in this case, skip the next step of selecting the fullscreen Canvas).

Select the checkbox for 'Add a Fullscreen Canvas'. You will be given three templates – choose one that you want to use and then click on 'Use Template'.

Next, add images, text, videos and the destination URL to the selected template.

You can see your created Canvas by clicking on Preview on Mobile.

Once done, click on Done and then click on Place Order.

You have created a canvas using an existing template. Now that the canvas ready, you need to know how to create the Canvas Custom Audience.

Navigate to Audiences and click on the drop-down menu to create a new Custom Audience. Select 'Engagement on Facebook' from the available options and then click on 'Canvas' as the type of engagement you want to use for this audience. Once you select canvas as the type of engagement, you will be taken through a similar process for creating a Custom Audience.

- Select the canvas with which you want the audience to engage
- Include – select an action from the drop-down menu that will tell what type of users will be considered
- Duration (up to 365 days)
- Audience name
- The description that should be optimized to tell the audience what you are trying to offer

When you select 'Include', you will be given two options – People who opened this Canvas and People who clicked any links in this canvas. If you choose 'People who opened this canvas', you will be targeting a larger audience as it will include all those who opened the canvas whether they did something after opening it or not. If you choose 'People who clicked any links in this canvas', you would be targeting a smaller audience.

You have created the Canvas Custom Audience, next is how it can be used. Each type of custom audience has its own maximum duration – a Website Custom Audience has a maximum duration of 180 days, a Lead Ad Custom Audience has a maximum duration of 90 days. Video Custom Audience and Canvas Custom Audience have 365 as the maximum duration. This is because the requirement for each type is different and a user is included in the audience if he takes the desired action within that time frame.

Thinking about how this can be used to reap maximum benefits, you can use Canvas Custom Audience to create a sales funnel. You can create a canvas to tell your users about your brand, a story, about your product and so on. Those who open the canvas will be added to the Custom Audience, and then they will be taken into the funnel. However, the biggest mistake some advertisers do is they take a shotgun approach, which means they target the ads with an objective and if the target audience does not perform the desired action, they are rejected. This is not the right way of creating a Custom Audience. You must understand that if a user has shown initial interest, you should keep him engaged even if he didn't convert initially. If he opened the canvas, it must have been for a reason. If he didn't buy, it must be for a reason. So, analyze and try to understand the problem. Show him another ad to keep them engaged as he might like and convert.

Chapter 5:

Facebook Events

Social media has left no stones unturned and has been a game changer in the world of advertising. The tools provided by these social media channels have enabled advertisers to adopt new ways to extend their reach in the global marketplace without spending too much money. Facebook has been working hard to find different ways to keep you connected with your friends and to find out what they have been up to. In this quest, Facebook created a tool called Facebook Event – a perfect tool to get attention from the users and manage it.

Planning and managing events can be a real challenge considering the fast-paced life we are leading. Facebook understands this well and that's why it came up with the concept of Events to make the job simpler for us. Facebook Events bring people together from different parts of the world. When you create a Facebook Event, you can connect with more people to empower them to spend some time with you to understand your business better. Using the calendar connection of Facebook, most people connect their smartphones with their Facebook Events, which means you can stay connected with your audience without putting in too much effort.

Use Facebook Events

Facebook Events emphasize the value your money holds, and that's why it is considered to be one of the best ways to spread the word about your brand, your product, your services, and your business. Facebook offers an Event, which is a free page that helps you interact with others and promote an upcoming occasion, such as sponsored gatherings, product launches, corporate celebrations, marketing events etc. It is a page that has its own discussion board, videos, photos, and so on. You can invite your friends to attend the event you have created by event invitations. These invitations are different from other types of invitations as it asks the invitee for an RSVP.

When you create an event on Facebook, you can invite your friends to that event. If your potential customers are your friends on Facebook, this is great as you can directly invite them. If they are not, the alternate option is to create a public event. By creating a public event on Facebook, you can invite any Facebook user to your event. You can change the setting in the upper-left corner of the dashboard to make the event either Private or Public.

Another benefit of creating events on Facebook is a notification is sent to the people who are invited to the event. You can prompt the user to respond to your invite by either saying they are interested or they aren't. Once they respond to the invite, the event appears on the calendar and their RSVP of whether they are "attending" or "interested" will be shown in the News Feed of their friends. This way you can extend your reach to the friends of your friends. If they are also interested in your event, they can join it.

Here's an example. While you were browsing through your Facebook Page, you came across an update from a friend that he is attending the "Decoupage Bottle Art" workshop in a nearby location. You too love art and wish to learn how to decoupage bottles. You check the details – the location, who is conducting the workshop, how many people are interested in attending, and then you too click on "Interested" showing your interest in this event. Now, you are a new customer of this art workshop. So, look at the power of this Facebook Event. The organizer created this event, your friend, who happens to be connected to the organizer, showed his interest in this event, it appeared in your timeline, and you got to know about it. That's the power and reach of Facebook Events.

As well as notifying people about the events that their friends are interested in, Facebook also shows that event in the suggested events for the person's friends. How this works is – using its intelligence, Facebook suggests events to a person based on the hobbies they have mentioned in their profile, their likes, the places they have checked-in, apps they use on Facebook, and the events they are linked to through their friends. This helps both you and your friend. You as the business owner benefit because your event is being shown to the right set of people, and your friend is happy that he is being notified about the events he might be interested in. Job accomplished successfully! The credit goes to Facebook as it is making the suggestions based on the user's behavior and network.

Another great thing about Events – Facebook suggests events happening near you that you might be interested in. In addition to notifying and suggesting events based on its intelligence, Facebook takes it one step further and notifies the users about events their friends are interested in/are attending that are happening in a location near them. Being friends, the person who is notified might be interested (sharing common interests).

Another reason to use Facebook Events is you can add a location to your post, thereby increasing the awareness of the event. When you create an event, you want more and more people to know about it, and who knows it better than Facebook! Facebook being a champ in spreading your message, helps you improve the visibility of your post in real-time. You can add your location and post pictures of your event in real-time to attract people. This will help you in the following ways:

- You can broadcast what's currently happening at your event to increase awareness.
- You can create more enthusiasm for the attendees when they know the event is going live and they might want to come to your next event too.
- If your event is happening in an approachable place, you might tempt some more people who are staying nearby to join.
- It might help someone who is randomly searching for things to do in his area. If you have tagged your location, and if that user is interested in the event, he might join you.

These days, most of us rely on our calendar to remember important dates, such as birthdays of our family members, friends, their anniversaries, wedding dates etc. With the kind of lifestyle we have today when we all are busy with our hectic schedules, we need apps for everything – whether it is booking a cab, booking a salon appointment, or remembering birthdays and events. Facebook is killer at this. It knows how quickly people forget about the events they wanted to attend, so it sends automated reminders to them when the event is around the corner. This helps attendees to remember the date and helps you to increase the attendance rate at the event. Another great way to promote events is through follow-up emails. They run email campaigns reminding people about the event and how they should attend. Once the event is over, they send emails to ask for feedback etc. Sending emails is a great way to remain connected with your target audience but what if those people are not reading emails often. An email reminder is easy to ignore, but a Facebook reminder is not. It will just pop up on the user's screen and appear as a notification.

Another benefit of using this feature is Facebook creates a forum for each event where you can connect with all the attendees. In this forum, people can like the event, connect with other users, and share their comments about the event. Being the event organizer, you can also use this forum to make announcements as it is a platform where all your attendees are present. So, if you want to update them about the location, the dress code, the guests who are going to join etc., this medium will come in really handy.

Last, but not the least, Facebook Event helps you keep a tab on the number of people who attended your event. The Event attendance tracking feature helps in several ways:

- It makes it easy for you to keep tabs on the headcount, which is an important metrics to measure your performance as well as to plan the next event.
- You can also keep a track of all those who said they cannot attend the event or responded in a 'Maybe'. This number is also important as it helps you review

your overall plan. You can derive several things from this – which age group is declining more frequently, females or males, etc. This data then helps in deriving several conclusions that help you in re-evaluating your target audience and you can see what you are doing wrong and if you are targeting the right set of audience for your events.

You can see the multi-fold benefits offered by Facebook Events. They are really simple to create and help you in expanding your reach to a larger audience without spending anything.

Creating a Facebook Event

It is not just about creating great events. You must understand the tool properly so that you can use it in the best way to plan, spread awareness, and coordinate.

In order to create an event – public or private, follow these steps:

- Browse through the left menu of the News Feed and click on Events.
- Now click on '+Create Event' from the left pane.
- You will be given an option to either create a public or private event. You must decide the type of event at this point as once it is created, you cannot change it.
- If you want to create a public event, set yourself or any of the Facebook pages you manage as the host.

- Fill in all the required details, such as Event Name, description, location, and time. If you have decided to create a public event, you can add additional information, such as – adding keywords related to the event, adding multiple dates as well as times, choosing a category for your event, and adding a link to the ticketing site for your event.
- Once you enter all the information, click on Create. This will create the event and take you to another page where you can upload images related to the event, invite your guests, add posts, and also edit the event information you just added.

You have created the event, but you must make it stand out so that you can attract your target audience by making it look great and catchy.

Choose an attractive image or video: Visuals are always more appealing than the normal text. They compel people to find out more about what's happening. While you may write about what your event is all about, try to represent it with an appealing image or video. If you choose to add an image, ensure it is of good quality (at least 1920 x 1080 pixels). This is important because images with a smaller ratio do not appear very clear and tend to be cut off. Also, avoid adding any text in the image so that it remains clear. Facebook ensures this by rejecting any image that has more than 20% text in it.

Choose an Event Name that is short: Having long names for an event can be a turn-off and the tool will not be able to accommodate the characters if it is too lengthy. The name needs to be exciting, fun and catches the attention of people. Remember, the name not only helps the event to grab attention, it also helps it stand out so that people are motivated to know more. Always avoid using caps and symbols that are difficult to understand – it should be simple, easy to understand, yet catchy.

Add a location: This will improve the visibility of your event. Adding a location that corresponds to a suggested location on Facebook helps attract the attention of more people, especially the ones who are nearby. You can either enter the complete address of the location or just the venue name (if it is recognized by Facebook, just typing the first few letters will autocomplete based on the option you chose from suggested options). This helps users as they can hover the mouse over the set location and see the details about that place. This way you are also promoting that venue (you can reach out to them and see if they can also promote your business as this way they are also getting more visibility).

Set the date and time: Doing this solves two purposes – the users know the exact date and time of the event, and add the event to their Facebook calendar so that required notification can be sent when the event approaches (this might increase the headcount as certain people just miss events because they do not remember the date and time). Also, for events that last for more than two weeks, it is recommended that you create separate events with specific dates and time.

Provide a description: The event description is some of the most important details of your event, such as what the event is all about, main motive (for example – charity, if you are organizing a charity event), the schedule, guest of honor, pricing etc. If you want to make it look more attractive, you can go a step further and do copywriting to attract a greater audience. Make the description search engine optimized by using relevant keywords. This will get your event listed in the search engine's results when somebody searches for something related to your event. Make the description as impactful as possible.

Optimize your event with keywords in Tags section: Never use only the brand name in the tag; try to use other keywords that relate to your Facebook Event. Here's an example. If you are hosting a fashion show, use "FashionShow" in the tag. Facebook will help you by giving suggestions when you start typing – so take help from the expert. This will help Facebook in recommending your event to people who might be interested based on their interests and likes. It helps if you add as many relevant keywords as possible.

People can post on your wall. When you are creating a public event, Facebook gives you an option to allow only the host to post on the wall or to allow everyone to post on it. If everyone can post, all the posts will first go to admin and only those approved will be posted on the wall. It is recommended that you do not select either of these options unless you have specific requirements. This is because when people are not allowed to post on the public event page, it is difficult to motivate them and the page looks very dull. Allow them to spark the conversation to make the event page look active. The more active the event page is, the more interested the audience will be and most likely to attend it. Allowing them to post on the wall also opens up a means of communication; they can use this channel to ask questions and the information you provide might help others who have similar questions. As the event organizer, you must respond to these queries proactively and also address the comments.

Pinning a post to the wall: Some people believe pinning can only be done on Pinterest, but that's not true. You can pin content to your feeds on Facebook. If you want to highlight something, you can pin posts on the top of the event page so that it is the first thing seen when someone visits the wall. You can pin update posts, start a countdown, or make an important announcement regarding the event. Pinning a post is very simple. All you need to do is click on the arrow that appears in the published post on the event page and click on "Pin Post".

Advertise your event: Creating an event will not help you get all the required attention, you need to advertise it. You need to spread the word in and out: In – within your circle, and out – in your extended network. Run Facebook Ads and place them where interested people see them. Advertise them just the way you do your posts so that it gets more views. This will help you in promoting it to those might be interested in attending, but are not aware of your business. Also, you shouldn't run your ads only on Facebook. Not all your target audience will be active on Facebook, so run your ads on other social media platforms. No doubt, the Facebook Event page will be the hub for all the required information, but this can be shared across the social channels by:

- Creating a story on Snapchat to promote your Facebook Event.
- Scheduling Tweets to send updates about your Facebook Event. Include the link to the Facebook Event in these tweets.
- Adding a link and images to this Facebook Event in your Instagram profile.
- Creating a Pinterest board and pinning the content of the event.
- Uploading a promo video on Youtube and other video sites.

You can also track the performance and from where you are getting the traffic by using a Bit.ly link.

Being the host of the Facebook Event, you can invite your friends to an event that is already created.

- Browse through the event page.
- Right below the cover photo, there is an Invite button. Click it.
- It will give you an option to choose the Facebook friends who you want to receive the invite, or you can invite them by sending an email or text message.
- Select the friends and click Send Invites.

You can also include more hosts to the event.

- Click Edit that appears on the top right side of the Event page.
- Click 'Add Friends' next to Co-hosts and enter the names you want to add as co-hosts.
- Click Save.

Hosts and co-hosts have the authority to invite people to the event and they can also edit the details of the event page.

Event's Story

Facebook combines the concept of storytelling (which is also available on other social media platforms) and event creation with the help of something known as an event's story. A story is a way of sharing some important and valuable information with other Facebook users who are interested or wish to attend an event. The story you add to the event will be visible for exactly 24 hours and after that, it will not be available. To share your event story:

- Browse through your News Feed and swipe right.
- Go to the bottom of the screen and tap a square button to take a picture or record. If you do not want to use visuals, you can tap on the text icon and add the content.
- Click on the right arrow button and then click on your Event Name to which you want this story to be added. You can even create a post, share an existing story or send to certain people on Facebook.
- Click on the blue right arrow key.

The event story will be visible with your event. Those interested or who have marked his status as attending or maybe can add a story to the event. If you are the host, you can approve these and post them on the event's storyboard.

Customizing your Facebook Event Page

You can also customize your event page on Facebook using some of the creative tools. If you have an event that keeps happening either daily, weekly or monthly, you can customize it by setting the frequency of occurrence. This way you do not have to create the event again and again. You can set frequency by:

- Browse through the Frequency tab on the Event page. From the drop-down menu, select just once or recurring (daily, weekly etc.).
- Now click on Custom and select the date when you want it to occur.

- Once the dates are selected, add start and end time for each of the selected dates. You do not have to do this for each event manually. Once you set the start and end time for one event, and if it's the same for other events also, just click on the box "Add this time to all the event dates".
- Click Done.

If the event you have set up on Facebook is a live concert that is being held in different cities, you can create the event as a tour. To create a tour on Facebook Page:

- Click on the Event.
- Select "+Create Tour" and add all the relevant information to this tour, for example – the name of the tour, photos etc.
- Now add events to the tour by clicking on "+ Add Events". You can now add all the existing events if you have already created them individually. If you haven't, you can create new events on-the-go by clicking on "Create New Events" and entering all the information for each of the events created. Save your event after each event is created and then move on to the next.
- Save the tour and publish it in the Events tab.

Remember you cannot create a tour without creating events, and when you publish a tour, even the draft events are published along with it.

Ways to Promote Your Facebook Event

Billions of people use this platform today to connect to things that matter to them. Get them to your event and create an engaged community by promoting your event. You need to drive awareness if you want your event to be successful.

Highlight It on Your Page:

You must highlight the Facebook Events on your page by:

- Shuffling your tabs and moving the event tab up. This will make it easy for your audience to find the calendar on your page. If your event tab is still not visible, then you can try creating an upcoming event.
- Your events should be visible on your timeline. While configuring the settings, make sure you select the Publish New Events to Timeline from the drop-down menu of the Events tab. This will automatically post all your events on your timeline.

Engage With Your Audience Using Your Events:

You can use your event to interact with your target customers by:

- Sharing the event on your Facebook Page so that you spread the word. Go to the Event and then click on Share button. Share it in News Feed to create awareness and interact with your customers by posting updates and having conversations.
- Ask your co-hosts and friends to share the event with their connects to create a buzz. Facebook provides you

a platform to involve several people in your event, so why not take advantage of that feature.

- Keep your customers engaged by regularly sharing updates and posting images and videos. When the event date is approaching, regularly sharing updates and visuals keep the motivation high. This way you can constantly connect with them so that they do not lose touch with you. People like to see regular updates on what's happening and this keeps them motivated. During the event, post updates and live videos to keep the excitement going. Going live keeps your audience encourage and also excite others to attend your upcoming events. Post-event, encourage others to share updates and their experience, thank them for coming, and promote your upcoming plans.

Make Sure Others Can Locate You:

You can help people who stay near your event location to discover you by adding your current location when you create an event as there might be people are close and would be interested in attending.

Advertise Your Event:

You can also create an ad to advertise your event to increase awareness and drive more traffic to your event. Facebook offers an option to optimize these Event Ads to generate event responses and sales on your website.

- **Create Ad campaigns** to drive awareness and generate interest. The ad objective for this campaign should be to drive awareness, generate interest, and retarget the important audiences. To drive awareness, announce the launch to create a buzz among people.

This should be done when you start selling the tickets. Take all relevant steps to keep your past attendees informed. Offer premium experiences, such as giving parking passes or VIP coupons. To retarget key customers, create last-minute buzz by sending promotional emails asking people to attend.

- **Target more effectively** to generate positive results by using Ads Manager. Your target should be all those who have responded to your upcoming or past event and their friends. You can also use Ads Manager to create a list of all those who have bought tickets for any of your events in the past. Create a list of all such people and similar based on the data that you have provided Facebook at the time of creating a profile (Lookalike Audience). Another thing you can do using Ads Manager is creating an Event Engagement Custom Audience by connecting with all those who have shown an active interest in your event.

Selling Tickets Through Ads:

You can improve the visibility of your event through ads and drive more traffic to your ticketing website. This should increase the ticket sale.

- Browse through the event page and click on Boost Event. Now click on Increase Ticket Sales. You can use targeting based on demographics. You can also include the URL of the ticket sales website of the event.

Managing the Events

Managing the events is as important as creating them. To effectively manage your events:

- /check all the posts that go on your event for quality by either allowing only the host to post on the event page or approving all the posts before they are published. This way you can check the content and post only what is relevant.
- You can save drafts of your event before they go live in public on the event page. All the saved drafts can be accessed through the Events tab present on the page.
- You can always schedule your events if you know about the start and end date. This way you can control when an event goes live. If needed, you can always go back and edit the settings.
- You can edit the information around the event any time before it goes live, but once it begins, you cannot edit it.
- You can use engagement, awareness, ticketing, and Audience Insights to see the level of awareness and engagement of your event. Browse through "View All Insights" on the event page to see how the event is performing organically and with the help of ads.

Chapter 6:

What are Facebook Places

In 2010, Facebook rolled out its location feature and named it *Facebook Places*. It is a location-based application that allows Facebook users to check-in using the Facebook mobile app so that connects and friends know where they are currently and what they are doing. Empowered by GPS, it provides the real-time update of a user's exact location even when they are on the move. It also allows users to take advantage of coincidences, such as finding out that you are watching the same movie in the same theater at the same time, or eating in the same restaurant as your friend.

Facebook didn't invent this feature as it was already being used by apps like Gowalla. When Facebook launched it, as Facebook was more popular, most users learned the meaning of "check-in" only when Facebook came up with this concept. People check-in when they reach a place, and when they do so, an update is published on their timeline. Users can also tag people they are with as well as their live video or images. You can also leave your review comments and tips that might come in handy when your friends show interest in a place or movie. If you didn't like a restaurant because of slow service, you can post that information with your check-in for the benefit of others. Although it is most useful to the younger crowd, even the middle-aged people seem to have been liking and using it.

Regarding your privacy, there are various aspects of Places that get turned on automatically so the user has to explicitly turn them off again. Whenever you check-in a place, your check-in update is published to your profile, your activity stream for that specific location, and your News Feed. Whenever a check-in is made, Facebook automatically includes you in the list of locations that are tagged as 'People Here Now', and your friends can see if you are present in that location without your permission. If you do not want this to happen, and if you want Facebook to show your presence in a place only when you allow it, you need to opt out of the default setting so that you can control what and how much information is available to other users about your location.

While Facebook has been emphasizing the fact that Facebook Places has been designed to make it easier for you to stay connected with your friends, and so others know where you are, some people feel it is infringing on their privacy. There are debates about the online privacy with the use of apps, and some users criticize the platform for this. Due to Places, there were allegations that the privacy settings are really complex and that the platform features opt-out mechanism instead of opt-ins, as some of the features on Facebook follow this trend. However, there will never be any issues if a user uses the feature the right way. For an example, in the case of Facebook Places, only the friends of a person will be able to see his check-in update, and not others, unless he explicitly makes his updates public. The game is always in the hands of the users. If the user knows the rules of the game and understands it, there won't be any issues. A user can choose to show his location update only to a certain group of people by changing the privacy settings accordingly. He can always choose to opt out of being present in a place by unchecking the box "Include me in *People Here Now* after I check-in" in the settings.

To control your location:

1. Log into your Facebook Account and browse through the Privacy Settings
2. Click on Customize Settings that appears on the bottom of the page
3. The field 'Places I check-in', is by default set to 'Friends Only'. You can change this setting by scrolling down to Customize to include and exclude people from the list.
4. If you do not want anybody to know about your check-ins, click on 'Only Me' so that no one knows where you are. Although it doesn't make any sense to check-in and change the setting to 'Me Only'.

How to change 'People Here Now':

1. Log into your Facebook Account and browse through the Privacy Settings
2. Click on Customize Settings that appears on the bottom of the page
3. You will see an option that says 'Include me in People Here Now after I check-in', so select it if you want to be included in that list and uncheck the box if you don't want others to see your location.
4. The status 'People Here Now' is OFF by default, so you are not listed in the People Here Now list. If you want to be listed, click on Enable.

If you do not want others to check you in a place:

1. Log into your Facebook Account and browse through the Privacy Settings
2. Click on Customize Settings that appears on the bottom of the page

3. Look for 'Friends can check me into Places' under the tab 'Things Others Share'
4. You can enable or disable this feature by checking the option 'Select One'

Create Facebook Places

Now that you understand how Facebook Places works, you can appreciate the power of this location-based app. You might want to use it for the benefit of your business. You could set up your own Places page so that your business customers can share their real-time location with their friends telling them where they are and what they are doing. How can you set up a Facebook Place page and get it up and running? It is important to note the following:

- The Facebook Place page must be created either by the business owner or by the customer.
- You must claim it to be yours to gain control over the page.
- If you create a general Facebook Page and mark its category as Local Business or Place, it explicitly becomes a Facebook Places page and you don't have to create it separately.

The first thing to do is locate your place. When you have checked-in a place and someone else attempts to check-in, your Places page gets created. You can create a new Page as Business Local or Place. If this person's check-in is the first check-in that is happening at the location you are currently present, the person who wants to check-in can simply search for your location and click on 'Add' on his mobile app to create the Places page. Once it is created, you can claim it to be your Business Page.

This way there might be multiple pages created for you when you check-in to different places. So, you will have to claim multiple Places (but you can always delete the ones that are not relevant later). On the other hand, if you haven't checked into any of the places so far and if your business doesn't have any location associated with its name, you can create it. The simple way to do so is to create a Place using your mobile app and add it to your business. Once it is created, just check-in at that place and then go back to your Facebook account and claim that page. To be able to create a Place page, you must be physically present at that place as Facebook Places is a geolocation-enabled program, hence your current location is detected and updated on your places page. This is how you can locate your current position:

- Log into your Facebook account and search for your business name using your GPS-enabled mobile app. You can enter the business in the search icon that appears on top of the Facebook Page.
- If there is no Places page already created, create one now.
- Using your GPS-enable mobile app, add a Place to your Business Page.
- Click on Check-In and then key in the name of the place. You will be shown a map of your location on your mobile screen, click on the Add button and add the location. You have now created your Place.

Next, claim this newly created Places page:

- Log into your Facebook account and look for your business name. You can enter the name in the search icon that appears on top of the Facebook Page.
- If you already have a Place page for your business, just click it to view the page. It should be displayed below the Places category.
- Click the link 'Know the Owner?' from the left pane. Another option is to click the gear icon that shows up under the timeline cover image and select 'Is This Your Business?'. you might be asked to verify if you are the official owner of the selected location.
- Click on the verification box and then click 'Proceed with Verification'.
- You will be required to enter the business information. Enter all the details and click on Continue.
- You might be asked to enter some additional information to verify the authenticity of your business and you, the business owner. It can be a document-based verification or email verification.
- Once you have verified yourself as the business owner, click on Submit.

Once this process is complete, you have your own Place on Facebook for your business. You might have all the information contained in your Places page already in your Business Page, but when you claim for a Facebook Places page, you can manage several things, such as your contact information, your business hours, admins, and other settings that are visible to other users on the mobile device.

Facebook Places that are Unclaimed or Unmanaged

Facebook is always looking for various ways to make it a better place for its users. In this quest, it sometimes denounces some old features to make a place for the new attributes. Something new that Facebook came up with is Unclaimed Places.

Facebook has always watched for anything that's trending and growing so that it can keep pace with the trend. One of the examples of this is Instagram. When Facebook saw Instagram becoming popular and trending in the market, it absorbed it. Another example was of FourSquare. Facebook has access to everyone having a mobile to check-in at a place they visited. If the location had a related page, people were able to upload their images, videos, leave comments, and do other types of interactions. But if that place didn't have a place, Facebook tried a game here. It would then ask the person to create a new page for that place by entering some of the important data, such as its name, exact address, contact details, business category, upload images, and so on. This way that location will have an associated Facebook Place. Once the page was created, they had the permission to leave a review about their experience of that place.

This worked very well and businesses were adopting this method. Places were even being claimed by people. Today there are too many Places that are not claimed by the business it stands for. There are several such unclaimed pages available on Facebook that are tagged as 'Unofficial Page'. An unofficial page is created for a brand by entering basic information but isn't owned or claimed by someone representing from that brand. Anyone who is a representative of that business can claim it just by going to that page and clicking on 'is this your business' that appears below the cover image on the page. When you do that, you actually raise a request for ownership of that page. Once your profile is verified, you might be asked to submit some additional documents as proof of your identity and how are you related to that business. The information given on that page is not enough to validate your identity as the representative of that business, and Facebook can't just have anyone claim a page.

Sometimes users have to undergo this process even when they have a Business Page on Facebook. By claiming an unofficial page, the focus on your main page is lost. When people look for you on the web, they start following one of the pages they find associated with you. If this is the unofficial page, they do not get updates from you because no one is active on that page, it is just a medium to accommodate followers – that's it. The solution to this problem is to claim the page and merging it with another page you own. To merge the two pages, you need to be very careful as if it's not done properly, you might lose a lot of important data. Ensure that:

- You own both the pages; you are the admin
- Both pages represent the same business
- Both pages have similar names
- If they have the same physical locations, the mailing address for both should be the same

Once you verify all this, select the two pages that you need to merge and then click the button to merge. When you raise a request to merge, you will be asked to select the primary page and then the merged page. The primary page is your active page, which remains as-is, and the merged page is the one that was unofficial. The data for the merged page is transferred to the primary page. If there are followers of this merged page, they will be transferred to the main page. The username, images, reviews, ratings, and posts of the merged page will be removed. That's the reason you need to be really careful during the merge process as you cannot afford to have this data removed from your primary page. Double check before clicking on the final step. Once merged, the data for the merged page is gone forever and there is no way to recover it.

If you see a page that looks out of place but there is no option to claim it, this means it is already owned by someone but the owner either doesn't use it or is using it as a caricature of his business. There can be a few reasons for this:

- The user is someone trying to phish and con your users by offering them knock-off services or products or is a criminal.
- The user/organization created a Facebook Page for his/their brand several years ago and then completely forgot about it. The person left the organization and the new marketing head doesn't even know such a page exists.
- Someone from your business created a Facebook Places page and never told you about it and you are unaware of it.
- Someone from a franchise created it to represent the business as a whole when it could only be used for the specific franchise.

So, the page cannot be used by the business and is very unmanaged. Someone needs to find out how to regain control and transform it into an active page. Facebook offers a couple of options to make this happen:

- Try to reach out to the owner of the page. You can try connecting by sending them a message through Facebook or using the contact details provided on the page. If you are able to get in touch with them, they might just give it to you. But if you cannot contact them, report the issue.
- If you connect and they are ready to transfer the ownership to you, they need to add you to that page as the admin. Once this happens, they will no longer be the admin of that page. Although a page can always have more than one admin, you might not want them to be the admin and want to control the page all by yourself.
- If you couldn't connect to the owner of the unmanaged page, you can report it as a violation of your intellectual property rights. Upon reporting, Facebook will look into the issue and take appropriate action. This doesn't mean you will get the ownership of the page just like that; Facebook might choose to either suspend it till any further action is taken or just remove it. They will even try to contact the page owner and see if things can be resolved. If it is removed, you will not be able to use the username unless you get in touch with Facebook support team and raise a request to use that username.

Facebook even allows you to transform a Place page to a Non-Place page. This means you can change the category of a Place page if you feel the current category doesn't match the information it holds. If there is a Place page that consists of check-ins and maps but doesn't have any information that adds value to your business, you might just decide to not use it rather than merging it with another page or transforming it into something else. Before you decide to cancel it, you must know that it is possible to change the category of such a page. For this, you do not need any approval or help from Facebook; you can do it on your own. The steps to achieve this are:

- Browse through that Place page that you no longer need.
- Click on 'Information' that appears on the top.
- Select 'Edit Page Details' and select 'Categories' box as it allows you to add few more categories.
- Once these additional categories are added, you can select which one works the best for your page. However, you must know that upon changing the category of your page, you are changing some of its basic features.

  For example – Magazines, Products, Brands, Books categories can access the website link, short description, ratings, review system, and services list. Similarly, Television, Movies, and Music categories can access all the above-mentioned attributes as well as an added phone number and email address. Likewise, each category comes with its own set of features.

Business Benefits of Facebook Places

Facebook Places is a great tool for marketing your business. It is a way of integrating the power of Facebook with the ability of the user to share his check-in details in a broader forum. It is a powerful tool that helps you promote your business, market your brand and build your loyal customer base. So, if you can utilize Places efficiently, you can reap several benefits.

Promote your business: One of the key reasons why some of the location-based services are so popular is word-of-mouth marketing. Using Facebook Places, you can encourage your target audience to share their feedback and views about your Business Page, constantly connect with them to advertise your business, give special discounts to those who share their reviews and write posts about your business.

Special Discounts: Offer a special discount to all those who checked into your Facebook Place during their visit. This way you are motivating your target audience to do more and more check-ins to your Place.

Reward and Appreciate: Holding onto loyal customers is key to a successful business. So, appreciate their loyalty and give them reasons to stay connected to your business by giving them several benefits – loyalty points, loyalty cards, loyalty offers and so on.

Chapter 7:

Facebook Groups

There is a general belief that Facebook is only good to connect with friends, share facts and opinions across the globe, etc., and nothing more. However, it might surprise you to know that you may actually use this global website to promote your business in a marvelous way. All you have to do is to create a Facebook group of your own or become the member of a group that another person manages.

Joining a Group

At first, when you opened a Facebook account, you had this tremendous temptation to join as many groups as you could! This is because you felt a need to be part of a larger society, if not offline, at least online. As a result, you began your exploration of diverse groups using this particular platform for communicating with others.

Although you can set up your own group on Facebook to target would-be customers to your business, it would be better to be a group member of other groups for a while. The groups you decide to join need serious thought. Spend time to select those groups whose members seem to match your vision of target customers for your line of business. You will gain relevant information by perusing the mission description of a particular group.

Check if the group is a closed, secret, or public. If it is a closed group, an administrator decides whether the group should accept your request to join or not. If the group is secret, only group members can access the posts placed on Facebook. You will not even be able to find such a group on search engines. A public group is open to anyone and everyone. If the group is an open one, go through the rules, if any, for interacting with the group. You should find the rules in a specific post tagged to the timeline, or in the description area. If the rules suggest that you could be a perfect fit, request permission to engage with the group members. Sometimes, a group asks some entry questions to be answered prior to granting permission. Once the process is complete, your request goes to the review. Soon, you will either receive approval to enter the group or be rejected. It is all up to the 'executives'!

Suppose that your chosen group has welcomed you into its inner circle. Do not begin lively conversations immediately. Go through the posts on display, both older and newer ones. You may type different keywords into the 'search box' to discover posts relevant to your business, advertisements, etc. True, this is a group comprises of individuals who share a common interest. Yet, you must comprehend the manner in which the members ask and answer questions, dispense information, offer advice, or express opinions. There will be a specific tone to the conversations despite the diversity of the posts on display. Once you comprehend this, you should find it easy to interact with the other members of the group. Because of understanding how the group operates, you should also find it easy to enhance awareness of yourself, of others, and of how to attract business opportunities. Over time, you should find it easy to seek questions that grant you opportunities to exhibit your expertise in a specific niche.

You may give direct answers to these questions, offer your products/services as the best answers/solutions to the questions asked, or provide a link to a helpful blog post on your own website.

You may not realize it, but you are marketing your business in a very subtle way. By providing solutions to problems expressed by other group members, you are actually targeting would-be customers. As you present yourself as a regular problem-solver, your image will imprint on the minds of other members of the group. They will seek you out and your solutions, whenever they need answers. They might even tag you into their comments. At the same time, do not just confine yourself to providing answers. Create a FAQs sheet from whatever knowledge you obtain from reading different posts and questions-answers. Later on, your sheet will also aid you in creating original and innovative content for your potential consumers on your own website.

Creating your Own Facebook Group

Once you feel comfortable and have gained experience about how a group should function, you might consider launching your own Facebook group. This is essential so you can play by your own rules, and not to play by someone else's. Of course, this does not mean that you should ditch the groups that you have joined. All it means is that you add something of your own in order to expand your promotional tactics. Apart from advertising your business and brand on other-managed Facebook Groups, you will also be able to advertise them through your self-managed group.

Purpose

It could be that you desire to build a database of customers. Therefore, you create a particular circle wherein only your regular/email subscribers may enter. By using relevant prompts and posts to further their education about your products/services and providing them with inspiration, you establish yourself as an authority in your particular niche. Whenever you offer valid tricks, content, tips, or tutorials to help your members to better their own businesses and lives, they will thank you wholeheartedly!

Sometimes, you benefit by initiating a group to focus on a subject that interests you. It could relate to advertising for health concerns, the psychology of advertising, etc. This kind of a topic-based group will lure people with similar interests to request a place in the circle.

You may build a community around your services/products. Offer it as a bonus whenever someone buys something from your shop. This will help consumers feel special/exclusive, especially when you exhibit a willingness to train or offer any kind of additional help.

Type of Group

Closed: If you would like to improve the knowledge of your customers, a closed group could be the answer. This way, your tutorials will be safe. In fact, many business owners prefer to operate within closed groups.

Secret: Your business will stand out as an established authority if you opt for a secret group. Only approved members will be able to benefit what you provide them. Sometimes, it helps to charge a monthly fee to join.

Public: It might be best to stay out of the public eye when you are running a serious business. You never know when spammers will intrude and destroy your reputation through irrelevant content. However, if your aim is to create a community around your business, then a public group works the best.

The Process

After deciding the type of group you want to initiate, you have to actually create it. Open your personal profile on your Facebook Page. You should be able to see a "Create a Group" option on the left-hand side of the page. Select someone to add to the group, even if it has no name yet. This is essential, and you cannot skip it. However, since you are going to create a 'business' group, choose someone who will not spill the beans before you are ready to set everything into motion. After adding Mr./Mrs./Ms X, provide a label for your new group. You may add other people if you wish to, specifically if they are inclined to exhibit interest in your products/services. Mention your privacy setting – closed, secret, or public. When you are through, press the button for "Create," and you are through!

The members of your group must be aware of what exactly is going on in the group. There is a 'settings' option, which you may use for outlining details, such as the type of group, description, location, email address setting, web address setting, and tags. Select a reasonably sized (825 x 325 pixels, preferably) and relevant image, which will show up on the timeline of your group. Click on it and describe the focus of your group and all the rules related to membership on the web page. You may place the rules at the top of the timeline where it is instantly visible. As soon as you decide that the group looks exactly the way you wanted it to, you may save the settings via another button.

Despite your vivid description, people may still want to know why you created this particular group and who is eligible for entry. Take time to create concise and interesting posts. Around three to five should suffice for the time being. Ensure that whatever you publicize, it must be entertaining, inspirational, or educational in nature. Only then, will group members feel like joining a discussion. In fact, it would be good to develop a long-term strategy for presenting novel content all the time. You may seek the help of websites, such as Entrepreneur, Google News, Buzzsumo, etc. and use links to trending content in the virtual world. Use the search engines intelligently to find interesting articles. Remain updated always, for you are a businessperson. Furthermore, when you have the latest information readily available, you will find it easy to comprehend and comment on opinions and viewpoints offered by other group members. You will even be able to offer great answers to various questions.

Adding and Engaging Members

It is always good to run through a list of familiar names and faces first, before moving on to mere acquaintances, or even strangers. Some of your personal pals will prove to be a good fit and hit with your group and you need to ask them to join your group. At the same time, please remember that family members and close friends may not prove to be 'paying' customers. They generally provide moral support and nothing more. Therefore, you have two options in front of you. You may retain them in the group and hunt for new members as well. Alternatively, you may opt to seek would-be-customers, who would find your products/services valuable.

There are several ways of sending out invitations. For instance, you may display an invitation on your web page, which casual visitors will be bound to see. Then again, if you have email subscribers to your official website, you may suggest that they join your Facebook group. Do not forget to provide a link to this page. In actuality, you may go one step further by displaying this link on all the social networking websites that you visit often. If you are tech savvy, you may consider placing a social button on your official website. The minute someone presses this button, they will have to move to that page on Facebook where your group's details are readily available. Finally, have a thank you page associated with your lead magnet and place an invitation to join your Facebook group on this particular page.

It is not enough to invite people to join your group and leave it at that. You have much more to accomplish! For instance, you will have to ensure that group members do not remain passive observers. They must learn to interact with one another. Toward this end, therefore, you will have to provide content that will spark comments, exchange of views, and questions.

1. One such content can relate to tutorials. Whenever you set up a tutorial, you are conveying the idea that you have expertise in a particular area. Therefore, you are a leader. Each video must provide support and help to the group members.

2. Another way of interacting is through question-answer sessions. Once in a week, have live 'shows', wherein you resolve problems as fast as they are presented to you!

3. A third way is to create an opinion poll every month. Ask your group members to vote for the content that you will provide in the subsequent month, the title of a blog, logo, etc.

4. Now, decide what kind of product/service you provide. Create a challenge to it. Invite the group to take up the challenge. When the challenge is resolved, members may opt for one-to-one meetings, wherein you move their learning to a higher level.

5. Everybody loves quizzes. You may use them to garner data from the members of the group. Alternatively, you may design a quiz so that your group members come forward with suggestions on what your next service/product should be.

6. Set up a prompt for a theme day. It should encourage individuals to share information about what they are doing on this platform. If the prompts are interesting, every member of the group will look forward to them. You might keep a certain day as 'promotional day', wherein the members of the group display their latest product or blog post. Request these members to display photographs about your product or your place of business. They are bound to comply.

Handling your Fans

As you continue handling your Facebook group in all the best ways possible, you will feel more and more grateful to your fans within the group. They not only believe in you, but also in your services/products and vision. You can just imagine the wonderful publicity they will provide your establishment via word-of-mouth. You need not worry about what they say; it is bound to be positive always!

Considering they do so much for you, it is your duty to be equally gracious toward them. Make them feel 'loved' by sharing their thoughts with others, giving them gifts, re-tweeting, etc. It is also important to thank them via handwritten, or rather typewritten notes. They need to feel glad about helping you reach your goals and making your dreams come true. Quite often, monetary rewards hold far less value than appreciative words.

There are different ways to use this kind of group to your advantage.

To begin with, whenever you feel the necessity to produce a new feature through your product/service, request your group to give positive/negative feedback. Seek mentors within your group. They are experts who enjoy using your services/products and sharing their knowledge with others. Urge these mentors to look after new consumers. If you feel the need to do so, you could begin a separate group for mentors alone. Share news about your business winning awards or your establishment being mentioned in a highly popular publication. Give them information about your other social media accounts. If your business has an affiliate program, recruit affiliates from the group itself. Finally, drop subtle hints to your fans to spread the word in forums about what you have to offer. They are your 'loudspeakers'.

Handling Existing Customers

Every time someone buys your products/services, invite them to become part of your Facebook group by providing a link on the signup page as well as in the 'welcome' email. You can also provide a description of how you work via the About Me section.

If you want this group to thrive, set an example by cultivating an environment of generosity. Do not be stingy about forwarding tricks, hints, and tips with regard to the lesser-understood aspects of your services/products. Request the regulars to share their experiences about using your services/products. If you receive complaints, do not become defensive or arrogant. Thank the customer for pointing out the problem, admit that you were wrong, offer an apology, and give an appropriate time when you should be able to fix it. Even if you cannot be on your Facebook Page throughout different times of the day, whenever you discover a comment/question, provide an immediate answer. If you cannot offer a solution instantly, tell the person that you will look into the matter and get back to them soon. Be inclusive to make each member feel that he/she belongs to an exclusive club. Make sure that the group hears of all the promotions and deals associated with your business. Finally, whenever you find someone discussing your company on another social media, send the person an invitation to join the group.

Handling Customer Segments

It is imperative that you take a keen look at the kind of customers who step into your establishment and join your

Facebook group. Treat each member as unique. Find out about their anxieties. Check out if your services/products are meeting their needs adequately. It is possible that you discover customer personas that are quite different from one another. The difference could be language, diverse needs, countries etc. If the numbers are sufficient to warrant the formation of a different Facebook group for each, go ahead.

If you spend some time in observation, you should be able to create an ideal Facebook group to receive rich rewards in the form of long-term customer loyalty. As your group grows, you may not be able to manage everything by yourself, especially the monitoring of posts and comments. In this scenario, think about hiring a community manager. This person should be from within the group. As this manager tends to administrative tasks, you may use the time to focus on your weekly/monthly goals.

Chapter 8:

Facebook for Professional Networking

Increasing awareness and enhancing the visibility of your business is not an easy task. Hundreds of messages and tons of meetings/calls are required to build a good rapport with potential customers. Constant connection is needed so that your customers remember you and whenever they need anything related to what you offer, they reach out to you first. A level of trust is required in order to get more business. Although Facebook cannot be a replacement for those meetings and calls, it can help extend your reach to improve your business relationship.

Each one of us has our own way of using social media platforms. While someone likes to share their complete profile, others might want to just show the basic information. It is important to be very careful about what you want others to know about you and what not to reveal.

You can use Facebook as a professional networking platform.

The Appearance of Your Timeline

Ensure you customize your profile for better and professional networking. You can start with your profile image as it is one of the key parts of your profile. It is your unique identifier and the way people will know you. How you want to be seen and remembered should be something with a professional touch, yet looking friendly (keeping the Facebook's theme in mind). Once you upload an image, you need to do few more things with your timeline. This includes:

- The About section: This section is meant to describe yourself – what you do, where you live, what you like, what you don't like, your hobbies, what do you for a living, and so on. Try to be as creative as possible and use the words that best describe you.
- Cover image: It is the image that covers the top part of your Facebook profile. Choose something that represents you/your page. It is different from your profile picture as it appears only on your timeline whereas your profile picture is what appears when you comment, share, or write a post.
- Contact details in the 'About' section: This is the section where you can give your contact details so that people can connect with you. If you do not want to disclose your contact details, you can leave this section blank.
- Education and work details in the 'About' section: Fill in all your work-related information (current and past) and educational details. This can really come in handy when people are looking for others in a specific industry or if they are doing a course.

How to use the Platform for Professional Networking

Regarding Professional Networking, there are several things that need to be considered professionally and personally. The main theme and underlying concept of Facebook is to build personal connections – to connect with your old pals, your long-gone friends, and relatives. On this platform, people appreciate talking about the real things you are doing and the best way to make professional connects is also through regular people who do regular things. When you connect these two spheres of your life, you make real connections. That's what Facebook is known for. Most of the established businessmen on Facebook have built their connections based on real relationships. Customers prefer to buy things from their connections – people whom they know and trust. For professional networking, it is important to reach out and connect with other people who are experts in your niche; you can contact other professionals and build trusting associations. Facebook offers several ways and tools to make this happen. You can start by Liking and Share their posts or images, and have conversations on common topics. At the same time, the contact shouldn't be overenthusiastic as it is not sincere.

You can begin networking by having conversations and meetings. You can schedule lunch meetings and have a discussion over a cup of coffee as connecting with someone face-to-face has more impact and helps to build strong professional bonds. Once you meet the professional a couple of times, you can connect to social media channels to keep updated and connected. Everyone uses Facebook in a different manner. So, take care of the personal space of the other person and try not to intrude as that might lead to breaking the bond instead of building it.

One old-school, yet effective, way of connecting with a professional over Facebook is sending offline messages and commenting on their updates. Connecting casually through simple discussions without sounding overzealous keeps you foremost in a professional's mind. These discussions do not always have to be about your business; you can talk about random general topics that he might be interested in. You can talk about everyday life, and eventually even discuss some sensitive topics if you feel you have developed that kind of rapport. There will be times when you get opportunities to connect with them on a personal level – they might ask your opinion on a personal matter or problem. You must remember that your professional connects are also regular people like you; they have their lives, their family, and experiences they love to share. It is really okay to talk about things other than business. The goal is to always be in touch so that you are always there on their mind.

Facebook can also be effectively used to build connections with your professional peers. Using the contact list from your email account, you can then invite them to be friends with you on Facebook. This option is often preferred by various users as it offers them a more casual environment to connect with others. Importing the contact list is seen as one of the simplest and quickest ways to enhance your connections. All you need to do is upload the list of your connections and an invitation will be sent by Facebook to all of them requesting them to join you. Here is how you can import the contact list and send an invite to them:

At the top of the screen, click on the silhouette icon.

- At the upper right, click on the link that searches for your friends. Upon clicking the link, the friend's page will appear which shows the outstanding friend requests, option to import contacts from other platforms, ways to manage your friend's list, people you know but are not connected, option to look for your friends by typing their name, location, hometown etc.

- Select one of the options you want to use to upload your personal contacts. From the options mentioned above, select one to see more options. Select the one that you want to use to upload.
- To add contacts as friends, follow the instructions to access the data to add your friends.
- Using the 'Choose File' option, select the file that contains data of your friends (you just created) and click on Upload Contacts.
- Click 'Confirm' once the upload process completes to send you the invitation to all the contacts that were uploaded.

Another way to network professionally is by igniting a controversial topic. However, you need to really know your audience to take this risk as it shouldn't break the bonds you've established. The topic you choose should be based on your ad objectives and the interests of your target customers. For instance, if you know talking about politics will encourage your customers to comment and actively respond, and if you think this isn't a turn-off, bring it on. Be very cautious if you want to use this method and define the rules of the game with your customers. This is important as your posts shouldn't be censored.

Another way to grow your network is by creating stronger engagements as they are the key to networking. The more you can connect and encourage your customers to talk, the stronger your network becomes and the more people will get in touch with you. To promote more engagement, post something on your page every now and then. People like to read about the topics that they are interested in, and obviously, if you are connected to someone, you share common interests. Post updates regularly so that you are on the minds of your customers. As well as posting, comment on updates from others and like or share them as appropriate. Facebook uses News Feed algorithm to keep track of pages you like and share. Based on your interests and likes, it promotes stories from your connects, therefore if you share and like stories from a customer often, you will see more updates from that person. So, don't be stingy when posting on your Business Page; be generous and post generously. Don't discount posting on Facebook because of its friendly theme. You can always bring in facts in a fun and interactive way. Facebook will always encourage you to do so even when it is about your business and most users on Facebook like a friendly tone. So, engage more often and drive more traffic to your Business Page.

When you share your updates on Facebook, always remember that people do not like to read text-heavy updates, and visuals are always preferred over text. In this fast-paced life, no one will be motivated if you post long updates. Keep them short and crisp, and include as many visuals as possible. Short updates that are embedded with images and videos are more effective as they catch the attention of other people. If a short piece won't do justice to the post, you can always share the link. This way, all those who are interested will check the link for more details.

When you are trying to build a community, try to be a part of that community so that you build it the most effective way. Having just another Business Page doesn't help you connect unless you give your customers reasons to take the time from their busy schedule to visit your page. If you want their time, you should first invest time in them. If you want others to read your posts and share it with their connects, start reading and commenting on their posts. The bottom line is – if you want to build stronger bonds, engage more.

How to Network Using Your Business Page

If you want to network in a more professional way, you can use your Business Page to engage with your target customers and keep your personal timeline aside. This doesn't mean you shouldn't be active on your personal timeline, you should still post but you can use your Business Page to network with your business partners or professional connects.

How to introduce and share your Business Page with existing as well as new customers:

1. Log in to your Business Page through your personal account and browse through the admin panel.
2. Click on 'Build Audience'.
3. Select all those you want to invite by clicking on 'Invite Friends'.
4. Select and close.

You can search your friends from the complete list based on where they live, their names, the recent conversations you had with them and so on.

You can also share the page using the Share Page option on your Business Page. This option is available in your admin panel or Business Page. Click on 'Share This Page' to share it in a group, on your personal timeline, or a friend and so on. Select to whom you want to share it and click Share Page.

Another way to network using your Business Page is by inviting all your email contacts to like it. Follow these steps to do so:

1. Browse through the admin panel located on the top right side of the Business Page.
2. Click on Build Audience and then click on Invite Email Contacts.
3. Tap on the link that says 'Invite Contacts' for whichever provider you are interested in using for inviting your contacts.
4. Using the instructions given, upload the contacts file so that an invite is sent to all these contacts to like your Business Page.

Chapter 9:

Facebook Analytics – Analyzing What Matters

Your target audience might be one of the million users who log into Facebook at least once a day. If this is true, it's a good news for you as Facebook is a goldmine for all those who are looking to market their brands or services online. If your target audience is present on this powerful platform and the important thing is to reach them and ensure you engage with them on a regular basis so that they remember you and your brand.

There are some of important metrics on Facebook that can help you gauge the performance of your marketing efforts. Once you know about these metrics, you can see how these metrics can be utilized to create marketing strategies that work. Facebook tools can also be used to analyze and create reports. You need to first understand some of the important terms because you cannot measure something if you don't know what it is. Having a good understanding of these terms can help you deliver better results.

URL Tags to Measure the Impact of your Posts

If you want to really do something great for your business in terms of promotions and advertising, you will have to get insight into what is happening around the advertising. An amazing, yet underutilized tool to do this is URL tags. Also known as the UTM parameters, URL tags can help you measure the viral impact of your posts.

URL tags are the tags that are attached at the end of a URL to track and analyze the clicks on a link. The tags make it easier for you to know where these people were when they clicked the link and a lot more information.

To create URL tags, you need to know: your URL (which is the original link to your website), the campaign source (where the campaign is hosted, example Facebook), the Campaign Medium (how the campaign is being driven – email, promoted post etc.), the Campaign name (the name of your business, brand etc.), the Campaign Term (these are the paid keywords that are used to drive it) and the Campaign Content (the content that distinguishes ads). All this data is really important as it will be later used to identify activities happening with the campaign within Google Analytics. And when the required data is entered, Google creates the URL that can be used in the campaign.

Once the URL is created, you can share it with your Facebook fans (not paid, organically) before using it in the ad that is targeted to reach your website visitors, fans, and Custom Audience. After doing this, you can use Google Analytics to determine how many people clicked this link by using "Campaigns" and "Acquisitions" available in the side navigation.

Key Terms

Engagement: Engagement is THE most important thing in the world of marketing. Creating content is crucial but if you don't make it engaging, there is no point to that content. If you create the content but no one reads it, there's no point. Therefore, the key to create engagement is through quality content. Facebook isn't a platform for broadcasting; it is a platform that helps you engage with your potential customers. This can be clearly seen from some of the features Facebook possesses, such as the ability to click on hashtags, replying to others' comments, finding new content and so on. In simple words,

Engagement on Facebook = Facebook Likes + Facebook Shares + Facebook Comments

Facebook Likes gives you the number of times people like your posts. This indicates how often your content is being liked/not liked by your target audience.

Facebook Comments is the number of times people comment on your posts. For comments, not just the number but even the tone of comment tells you a lot about your post. Pay attention to the number of comments as well as the tone to understand what people feel about your products, services, or the brand.

Facebook Shares is the number of times people share your posts or content with others. This improves the reach of your post as it is seen by an amplified number of people.

Engagement is the ability of your brand to create a connection with your content or to capture the attention of your potential customers. It also plays a role in defining who sees your posts on Facebook because it is a key factor in News Feed algorithm. What posts are displayed on the News Feed and who can see it, is governed by an algorithm, and Engagement plays a key role in this algorithm. When people make an attempt to connect with you, the actions they take to create this connection appear on their timeline, and this makes their engagement actions visible to their friends. This is how your brand awareness improves.

Engagement is an attribute that defines your audience – what are they interested in, what they like, what they don't like, is there a segment of your audience that interacts more with the content you create and so on. All this information can come in handy when you are doing content targeting.

Engaged Users: Regarding the audience on Facebook, there are several factors that are more important than the number of fans you have on your Business Page. Engaged Users is one of those factors. Engaged Users is an important metric that tells you the number of people who actively engage with the content on your Facebook Page. In simple words,

Engaged Users = the number of users who actively engaged with your page and includes both the number of clicks and story generated.

This metric can be found at both post level and page level within the Facebook Insights tool. Engaged users are not just fans but also those who engage with your Facebook Page. Measuring this metric goes one step beyond calculating the number of fans of your page. It is calculating the number of people who took action on your page. The action could be a comment, a like, or share on your Facebook Page. Keeping track of these Engaged Users as a percentage of the total number of fans you have over a specific period of time can tell you whether you are creating an active or passive target audience. The more the Engaged Users, the more positive is your growth. If the number doesn't grow, it means your content is not being seen. If it does, it means they are consuming and sharing the content you post on your page. These users form the most valuable segment of your audience.

Engagement Rate: Engagement rate is the measure of your effectiveness at creating engagement in your audience. It is a metric that can give you insights into what kind of posts and content you should create to grow successfully. Engagement rate can be calculated in various ways based on the information available.

- If you choose to use the data of public posts, you can find and compare your engagement as a percentage of the total number of fans you have against other brands on Facebook using the Simply Measured Facebook Competitive Analysis.
- If you choose to use the Engagement Rate Metrics within Insights, you can easily calculate the Engagement Rate of your brand, whether it is for a single page or multiple.

You can compare the performance of your post or page against other brands using the public data on Facebook (the first option), and measure the accurate performance of your brand posts using the Insights data on Facebook (the second option).

Engagement Rate = People who Like + Comment + Share + Click on your post / People who Saw your post

You can calculate the Engagement Rate to measure how many unique users engaged with the content on your page as a percentage of total users who were exposed to it. Using the Facebook Insights data, you can know the unique user totals for engagement actions on the posts + overall reach of those posts. This way you can see that the Engagement Rate is much more than just liking, sharing, commenting, and clicking.

You do not need to use the Facebook Insights data to calculate your Engagement Rate against that of the competitors. You can still analyze it to derive important insights by considering engagement for both pages and posts as compared to a total number of Facebook fans. To calculate Engagement as a percentage of total fans, the Simply Measure Solution can be utilized to compare Engagement Rate of competitors to your own.

Engagement Rate = Total Engagement (Shares + Comments + Likes + Clicks)/Total number of Fans

How the Engagement Rate tells you about the quality of each post and you can know if you are targeting the right set of audiences. Engagement as a percentage of a total number of fans so that you can compare engagement on your Facebook Page with other competitor pages so that you can know the quality of your audience and see if the content you have is effective as compared to that of your competitors.

Reach: Another important metric that most of the marketers are bothered about is the total number of fans for their page. Although what matters most when you want to measure the quality of the audience is the number of people who are seeing the content and not the total number of fans.

Reach is the key metric or performance indicator that determines the number of people who are seeing the content.

Reach = number of unique users who are seeing the content on your page

There are different types of reach for your content – Paid, organic and viral.

Paid Reach is the number of unique users who see the paid content you use.

Organic Reach is the number of unique users who see the content on your page or News Feed

Viral Reach is the number of unique users who see your post or page and mention it in stories published by their friends. These stories could be in the form of comments, shares, likes, or responses to events.

If you measure Reach by type, it will help you determine the factors that made people see your content.

- If you see an increase in the organic reach, it might mean your fans or engagement has increased.
- If there is an increase in the viral reach, it can mean that your content was sharable.
- Changes in paid reach can mean your content was viewed because of ads you published on the network.

Apart from the types, reach can also be analyzed for the whole page or for individual posts. Reach for a post means how many people viewed your post whereas reach on a whole refers to the number of people who saw the whole page.

Reach gives you the measurements of the effective audience for your brand. It is more important than knowing the number of fans as not all fans of your page view your content, but all those who do, are important.

There are several factors that impact the reach of your content and the News Feed algorithm helps determine these factors. Who sees your content, which fans action on the engagement activities such as shares and likes – all this needs to be determined to improve the reach. You need to find out how to:

- Post content that can be consumed easily and quickly
- Increase engagement by growing the number of engaged fans on your page
- Reduce the negative comments on your page

Impressions: The most important thing and the biggest challenge for marketers on Facebook is making a mark into the News Feed of users. Impressions is a performance indicator that tells you how many times your post was seen and how many times users were exposed to that post.

Impressions = Number of times your page content was displayed

Impressions, just like reach, are of three types – Paid, Organic and Viral.

Paid Impressions is the number of times your content was visible on the News Feed or page of the users.

Organic Reach is the number of times your paid content was visible.

Viral Reach is defined as the number of times content associated with your post or page was visible in the stories published by users' friends. These stories could be in the form of comments, shares, likes or responding to events.

Some people get confused between reach and impressions as both are the performance indicators to measure the visibility of content for three types – organic, viral and paid. The main difference between the two is while impressions measure how many times the content is displayed, reach measures how many unique users saw it. For instance – if there are ten users and each of them saw the post twice, the impressions would be 10, and reach would be ten as 10 unique people saw the post.

'Impression' is an indicator of your ability to expose people to your content, which helps in determining how many people you are able to reach and how frequently they are seeing that content (content of posts or page).

There are various factors that impact the organic impressions and these factors need to be worked to optimize your marketing tactics. To increase the impressions, you must –

- Post content that can be consumed easily and quickly
- Increase engagement by growing the number of engaged fans on your page
- Reduce the negative comments on your page

Stories: Facebook Stories are updates shared by friends about their actions or engagement with a person, page, or event. The Facebook Stories of your friends will appear on your News Feed.

Stories = updates from friends regarding their engagement with pages, people etc. that appear on your News Feed

Stories are created when a user makes engagement actions, such as comments on a post or page, likes a page, posts something on a page, tags someone on a page, and other various types of interactions. You can view stories related to your business to see how effectively your content increases awareness for your Business Page. These stories can be segmented based on actions taken on posts or pages to understand the awareness of post content and page content. For instance, if you see there is a high volume of stories about a post, it could mean the post had some engaging content or was posted by an influencer.

Stories that are created by users about your brand posts are capable of driving awareness for your Business Page. The more people engage and see your page, the greater the chances that some of their friends will see a story related to it. When people engage (like, share, comment, or click) with your brand posts, details of how they engaged appears in the News Feed of their friends, and this is what a story is. For example, a user might see a message in his News Feed that his friend John liked ABC company's page or John commented on ABC company's page.

Consumptions: When people talk about Facebook, the only words that come to their mind are – Likes, Shares, and Comments. This is mainly because these are the key actions users take on Facebook and that's how most of the engagements are governed. These are also the key performance indicators that most of the marketers use to access how they are doing on Facebook. But trust me – Facebook is much more than these three keywords. If you look at Facebook Insights, it offers you wide variety of metrics to gauge your performance that goes beyond Likes,

Shares, and Comments. These are called consumptions. Consumptions are the clicks on your posts.

Consumptions = Clicks anywhere on the post – they can be the ones that generate a story or simple clicks

This metric can be seen at both levels – posts and pages, within Facebook Insights. However, these can be divided into:

- Photo views
- Link Clicks
- Video plays
- Other clicks, including Likes, Share, or Comments that generate stories

An important point is that consumptions do not include the scenario when a user Likes a page in his timeline. These consumptions don't even create stories in the News Feed as they are all about clicks.

Segmenting the consumptions can give you additional information about the type of content that is able to engage users on your page. It also provides the volume of other engagement actions that created stories. For instance, you can see how many people viewed your enlarged image on your post in contrast with the number of people who liked, shared, or commented on it. But most important is how these consumptions are important when they don't even create stories in the News Feed. When someone clicks on your post or page, the engagement action is stored in the algorithm the News Feed uses. This means by measuring the number of clicks on your post, you can get a better view of engagement and if your posts will continue to show in the News Feed of users. Additionally, when these consumptions are cross-referenced with other key performance metrics on Facebook, it can be extremely useful to measure the performance of your content. For instance, when you combine consumptions with impressions, you can evaluate the click-through rate for content for each type, and you can measure the frequency of the content.

Consumers: Consumers are they different from the Engaged Users. Consumers is another performance metric that is less known by marketers but it is something that can give detailed insight into content performance. Consumers is a metric that defines the number of people who clicked on any posts, whether that click generated a story or not.

Consumers = number of people who click on any of the posts (whether it generated a story or not)

They are the people who click on your posts, whereas Engaged Users are the ones who click on the page or create a story anywhere on the page (taking engagement actions – like, comment or share). Engagement by consumers is limited to only click on posts, while Engaged Users can click anywhere on the page. Engaged users on your page will always be equal or greater than the consumers. These two metrics – Consumers and Engaged Users – can be found within Facebook Insights for both posts as well as page levels, but for post level, the number would be the same.

Both Consumers and Engaged Users metrics give you insight into the content performance and the audience engagement on your page. There is a difference in how each metrics is calculated and used. As Engaged Users generate Stories by clicking on the page, it gives a complete picture of the engagement of your page, which makes it ideal to determine how engaged your audience is on the page. Since Consumers are limited to clicking only on the posts and not on the page, Consumers measure the performance of individual posts and can also be segmented to take different types of action and it gives a deeper insight into how a user engaged with your content and what type of post did he engage with – photo, video etc.

Like Sources: We all know what it means when someone 'Likes' your post on Facebook. Today, it is seen that more and more users choose to engage through these likes, which is a positive sign. When someone likes your page, that user is known to have become the Fan of your page. But sometimes, you need to do much more than knowing the number of fans you have for your page. You need to know how these fans find your content, and hence you need to analyze the Like Sources. These are the places where people can like your page. In simple words,

Like Sources = Places where people can like your page

The sources can be found with the Facebook Insights and can be segmented into different heads – On your Page, Page Suggestions, Ads and Sponsored Stories, Your Posts and Others. And each segment is divided further, within the Facebook Insights tool. This is because there are several types of sources from where your page can be liked. For example – Page Suggestions (people who like your page through a Page Suggestion invite from Facebook admin), Timeline (people who like your page through the Like section that appear on their timeline or someone else's), Ads (people who like your page by clicking on 'like' on an ad or sponsored story that points to your page), Registration (people you added as admins), Favorites (other pages you added as your favorites and they liked your page), Like Story (people who like your page from a story they came across through their friend who liked it), Ticker (people who like your page from a story they came across in ticker), Page browser (people who like your page by using the page browser of Facebook) and so on.

The list is not yet over as there are various other sources from where people can like your page.

These Like Sources can help you analyze how users are finding out about your page and liking it. it gives you an insight into how various sources get you more fans. For instance – the number of people who like your page from a mobile, how the external sources such as social plugins help you drive more users to your page and so on. This way you can make better-informed decisions and accordingly design your Fan Page.

Paid Likes: Most brands spend a portion of their budget on social media advertising and this form of marketing is trending. Marketers who advertise on Facebook should be able to segment their performance based on paid and organic activities. Paid Likes are the likes you get from people when they click on an ad you published or a sponsored story.

Paid Likes = number of people who like your page from an ad or sponsored story

Paid Likes can be found from Like Sources within Facebook Insights, which we discussed earlier in this chapter. The three sources of Paid Likes within Like Sources are – Mobile Ads, Ads,and Sponsored Stories. And the sum of likes from these three Like Sources gives the total number of Paid Likes for your Facebook Page. Knowing the Paid Likes helps you understand the returns on the amount you are spending on Facebook advertising. Depending on your growth, you can determine how to budget these ads on Facebook. However, the challenge of measuring performance on Facebook is not limited to just the Likes. Paid advertising also impacts reach, impressions, and engagement. When you analyze all these metrics, it's then that you will know the actual impact of advertising on Facebook.

Organic Likes: These are Likes on your page that are not linked to advertising you do on Facebook. These can be calculated by subtracting Paid Likes from the total number of Likes. You can segment the Like Sources to find out if the likes you got on your page were triggered by a third-party app or something else.

Now that you understood the key metrics, you need to start using them so that more informed decisions can be taken to improve campaign performance and achieve success.

Improving the Facebook News Feed Exposure

If you want to improve the exposure of your Facebook News Feed without using the Facebook ads, you can do it with the help of the Audience Optimization feature on Facebook. Facebook has given advertisers and business owners a huge audience set, but lately, the saturation point has been reached due to brand content, This is making it difficult for the brand owners to improve or achieve visibility in the News Feed of their audience and provide content that resonates with their needs. Using Facebook's Audience Optimization, you can easily and effectively target your posts to certain segments of your audience based on their behavior and interests. By doing this, you are creating an opportunity to tailor the content and optimize it for better engagement – both in terms of the subject and the flow. Here's how you can use organic post targeting to reach those specific parts of your page in a better way:

Step 1: Enable the Audience Optimization option for your posts by navigating to targeting icon. On your Facebook Page, compose a new post. You will see a targeting icon below the field that says 'Write Something'. If there is no icon, activate this by clicking on Settings at the top of the screen. Navigate to the General tab and click Edit for 'Audience Optimization for Posts'. You will be shown a pop-up screen, in that click on the checkbox that states 'Allow Preferred audience selection and the ability to restrict the audience for your posts'. Next – click on Save Changes. Once this is done, you should be able to see the targeting icon on your New Post compose page.

Step 2: Use the Audience Optimization option for published and New posts. Once the organic targeting feature is active on Facebook, you can start using it for new as well as already published posts. In case of new post, when you make an attempt to compose a post, click on the organic targeting option below it. You will see a pop-up screen with two options provided – Preferred Audience and Audience Restrictions. You can define your target audience segment on the basis of their age, gender, location, interests and more. So, go ahead and define your preferred audience first. Click on the Preferred Audience and select the people you would like to target in News Feed; these are the people who are more likely to view the post created by you. You can add up to 16 tags to define the audience based on their interests. This means when you add these tags, people who are interested in these, are more likely to view this post.

Facebook also provides recommendations around the tags, so you will see that when you start entering the tags, it will provide suggestions for other tags. You can use these suggestions or add your own tags, but what's important is to make informed decisions based on target demographics.

Step 3: Create Audience Restrictions to restrict the visibility of your content. The second option that was provided to you in the pop-up screen was Audience Restrictions. This works in conjunction with the Preferred Audience option. While Preferred Audience gives you the ability to define the tags that will help you to show your posts to an interested audience, Audience Restrictions allows you to control the visibility of these posts to only the select demographics. People who are not part of this select demographics will not see the posts you have created as they might not be interested in them. You can restrict the visibility of your posts based on gender, age, language, and location. For example – you can mention that your Facebook posts should be visible to only Americans between the age 30 and 60. Once you are done defining your targeting criteria, click on Save and then Publish the post.

Step 4: Analyze to see if your efforts are paying off

Now that you have defined your Preferred Audience and Audience Restrictions and targeted your posts to specific segments, it is time and analyze your efforts and determine the engagement of your preferred audience. Navigate to the Insights button on your page, and click on Posts in the left bar. This will show you your reach (Organic, Paid) and engagement of each of the posts. It also shows how many people have interacted with your posts and how many have comments, liked, or clicked on it. This will tell you the type of content that interests your audience. If you are not happy with the results, you can always return to this area and choose different settings/audience.

Facebook Insights

As much as it is important to know different features and attributes of Facebook, it is also important to understand how customers interact with your content. Another powerful tool is Facebook Insights for you to use to analyze the page administration to determine what updates are important for your audience and what are their valuable demographics. If you use the power of Facebook Insights properly, you will be able to understand your audience better, which will further help you to publish content that has value to them. Your ultimate goal is to better engage with your target audience. Facebook Insights gives you an insight into what your customers are looking for. The better you understand it, the better you will be equipped to serve them.

Facebook Insights is a tool that is specially designed for marketers to analyze their target audience to get information, such as demographics, shopping behavior and so on. Here's an example. You want to increase the awareness of your product – comfortable, high-quality yoga mats, which you have been selling in a store. To increase the sales, you want to improve the brand awareness by knowing how many people live near that store, their likes, their hobbies, their fitness goals, and their purchase behavior. You can get all this information with the help of Facebook Audience Insights.

Page Likes: this tells you the top pages people follow or like in various categories, such as fitness outfits.

Demographics: this gives you the information about lifestyle, age, gender, job role, relationship status, education.

Facebook usage: this tells you how often your target audience logs into Facebook and how they access it (mobile app or website).

Purchase behavior: this tells you about the past purchase behavior of your target audience and their purchase methods (online, store).

Location and language: this gives you information about where your target audience lives and the language they speak.

There are two types of Insights available on Facebook – Audience Insights and Page Insights. While Audience Insights look into the trends your potential customers are following on Facebook, Page Insights gives you information about their interaction with your Facebook Business Page.

Facebook Page Insights

With the Page Insights tool, you can peep into the life of your target audience – you can see what posts they are engaging with, what posts they like/do not like and so on. This data can help you make important decisions about the content you should publish on your page. It gives you an idea of what kind of content is best for your Business Page. When you know this, you can build a stronger audience base and have more and more people interact with you through your Business Page. People are always looking for information that can help them achieve their goals, so if you have it for them, they will stay connected with you.

Use Page Insights to see how your target audience is connecting with you on your Business Page. Click on Page Insights and you will see:

- The reach of your post and the number of people who engaged with your posts.
- The number of people who reached out to your business from your page.
- The number of times you responded to their queries or posts and your average response time.
- The number of times people checked your business through their posts.

Use Page Insights to understand what kind of content best resonates with your business theme. Click on Page Insights to see data to adjust your content in a way that you improve engagement and grow your audience base. You can do this by analyzing:

- **Reach**: how many people saw your posts and how many of them liked, shared or commented on them. It will also give you an insight into the posts that could get the most attention of the target audience, which will help you create more posts of that kind to improve interaction and engagement.
- **Page Views**: how many people are viewing your page and what exactly about your page they like the most – specific updates, posts etc. Once you have this information, gather the aggregate information on these people based on their gender, age, and location so that you can target other people with your boosted ads and posts, or tweak the content you have, to match their needs and interests.

- **Posts**: how each of the posts on your page has performed over the specified time – what is the reach of each of these posts, how many have responded with reactions and clicks and what's the type of posts that most of the people like. Using this information, you can see what's performing the best.
- **Actions taken on the page**: what actions people have taken on your page – if they are clicking on the Call-to-action button or clicking on the link that takes them to your website. Using this information, you can make changes on your page so that people take action that you want them to.
- **People**: information about location, gender, and age. You will see what is it on your page that people are looking at and how did they find it there. Using this information, you can create posts in a way that it produces the best results.
- **Likes**: location, age, and demographics of your target audience. For example, if there is a post on 'Cheap Flights Switzerland', using the graph you can see if the majority of the target audience includes males or females, where are they located, and accordingly you can tweak your posts. You can also search using unlikes. You can go back and see what went wrong on the days you have had 'unlikes', maybe too many posts without images.

No matter what you are trying to achieve on Facebook, or what your ad objectives are, these Page Insights will help you understand who among that group most interacts and likes what you have on your page. It is a powerful tool for all those who want to know user interaction on their Facebook Page. You will also be able to determine the best day of the week to the post, the best time of the day, and the best type of content. All this data is provided in the form of graphs on the Insights dashboard. Just below the graph, you will also have information about the latest posts and understand their virality as that helps you understand which posts are most liked – links, videos, all post types, photos, questions, platform posts, and posts.

Facebook Audience Insights

Facebook Audience Insights is another powerful analytic tool. It can be accessed through Facebook Ads Manager and is totally free. Audience Insights provides behavioral and demographic data of your audience as well as your competitors. This tool was specially created for marketers so that they can target their ads more effectively and efficiently. You can use it to know your audience so that you can improve your overall marketing strategy on Facebook by posting more compelling content, posts that attain stronger buyer response and more competitor research. This data is sourced from self-generated Facebook data and third-party data partners. The self-generated Facebook data includes the information given by users in their profiles – job title, gender, age, page likes etc. Some of the data including purchasing behavior, household income etc. are available through third-party companies that match this information to Facebook users.

How to access Facebook Audience Insights.

Step 1: Click on the Facebook Ads Manager and then from the left-hand menu, select Audience Insights.

Step 2: Choose your audience. You can choose everyone on Facebook to be your audience or create a Custom Audience.

You can also choose to select only the people who are connected to your page.

Everyone on Facebook – this would give you an overview of the entire Facebook. You should select this if you want to understand the data based on competition or broad interests.

A Custom Audience – You can create your own Custom Audience. If you already have a set created, you can use that here. If not, you can create one by uploading the email addresses. The platform will match these addresses to find the respective user accounts. This is especially helpful when you have a lot of data as it helps you analyze the behavior and demographics of the audience already using your services or brand.

People Connected to your Page – With this option, you can select your own pages from the list of pages displayed so that you can understand your audience.

Choose 'Everyone on Facebook' and set up other attributes.

Step 3: Select the parameters. You add characteristics that identify your audience. Some of the fields have values set by default, and you can change them based on your audience. You can also remove options from the list by just hovering over the option and selecting 'remove'. You can add and remove as many options as you want. You can also segment your audience based on factors, such as their interests, gender, age, people connected to you etc.

Step 4: After segmenting, you can explore the data to understand more about your audience. For instance, if your target audience is people in the US who practice yoga and are interested in it. Within this option, you have six options available that cover various aspects – Page likes, activity, household, purchase, location.

<u>Page Likes</u> – This tab can be divided into two sections. The first section is the top categories of pages that your select audience likes along with the top pages in that particular category. Taking the example of your yoga followers in the US, we can determine what they like on Facebook and find out more about their purchase behavior and interests. You might find that there are a lot of things they like and comment on including fitness centers, fitness brands, fitness products. You can also check if this list comprises of luxury brands or the affordable ones. The second part is the specific pages that this set of people is more likely to 'Like' than any other user on Facebook. Then analyze these pages to see what is it that your audience likes about these pages – content. This will help you understand the type of content they are interested in.

<u>Activity</u> – Activity is another tab that helps you understand the activities and behavior of your target audience. This tab comprises of two sections – Frequency of Activities and Devise Users. Frequency of Activities gives you the 30-day data showing your users' activities including the number of pages they liked in the last 30 days, number of engagements they made in the last 30 days and so on. Device Users option gives you the list of devices that your audience use to access Facebook - mobiles or website. This information will help you to understand how active they are on Facebook so that you can see if it's worth using it to connect with your audience.

<u>Location</u> – Within Location, you have an option to see top countries, top cities, and top languages. Since in our example, we have the data filtered for the US, the Top Cities

tab will show the United States. The top cities will tell you where in the US these people are located who like yoga. This should help you to understand if you are targeting the right audience.

Demographics – This tab includes information on gender, relationship status, job title, age, and lifestyle. This data comes in handy when you are trying to create content and personas to engage with the target audience. You can segment further to find data for your potential audience.

 Step 5: Once all the useful data is available, it can be used to understand the audience and create content accordingly. This data can be saved to create campaigns and other things by simply clicking on 'Save'.

Facebook Audience Insights tool gives you access to some of the valuable information regarding the target audience that can be used to learn their behavioral pattern and purchase behavior. This data can be used to create effective advertising campaigns, and build content that helps potential customers.

Basic, yet Important Analyses

There Is Much More Beyond Your Fans on Facebook.

When there is a need to measure your target audience on Facebook, there is much more beyond just knowing the number of fans you have. You can get more fans by attracting them through your special discounts and promotions and making them Like your page. But the fact that they Like your page, or are your fans, doesn't mean they are engaging with the content you are posting – which is what is important. Having fans that are not engaging with your content, will not help you. It is important for marketers to realize that it is impossible to steer the wheel of growth without actionable insights of their audience. To be able to analyze the audience, you must know:

- The type of content they like and engage with
- Build more engagement with your brand
- The people are you connecting

These are the tactics you must focus on to add meaning to your audience analysis:

1. **Who are you actually reaching**: Everyone who sees your content are not just your fans. Hence, knowing the number of fans won't give you the number of people who are actually seeing your content, and metrics that can give you a clearer picture of the effective audience. Knowing your reach at different times helps you understand how the content you post impacts engagement with your audience. Without knowing reach, you cannot measure your ability to attract people and convert them into potential customers.

   Reach is broken down into paid, organic, and viral. It is always recommended to measure each of these types separately as each gives you different things. While paid reach tells you the number of people who engaged through an ad and might help in driving awareness and sales for your product rather than just engaging with your community, viral reach indicates the quality of content you shared – if it was shareable. Organic reach indicates the audience that engaged with your content and more likely to drive engagement.

2. **Know about your Engaged Users**: Engaged users are the people who not only Like your page, they take engagement actions on your page, so it is important to grow their number. Having fans who are not Engaged Users will not help you; you need users who engage with your content and take actionable steps such as Like, Share, or Comment. As the number of fans grows, you also want the number of Engaged Users to grow. This metric is often coupled with reach to see how engagement is being driven by the content strategies used by marketers.

   While it is important to increase the number of Engaged Users, it is also important to understand how effectively you are engaging them. This can be done by measuring Engaged Users as a percentage of reach. This is important because if you are not effective in engaging those who are reading your content, you might lose your potential customers.

3. **Increasing the number of fans is important for community**: Just having fans, cannot achieve success; getting new fans is important for the health of your community. If you set the context right, it will help you increase the size of your audience. Analyzing Like Source can help you understand where the users were and how they were accessing Facebook when they liked your page. You can further segment the Like Sources to find out whether you could get these

fans from organic sources or paid sources. Organic fan growth indicates the fans you earned without the help of ads on Facebook. It also identifies tactics and events that helped earned these fans. It also gives you an overview of how digital sources are helping you drive growth – plugins and mobile apps.

4. **Make informed decisions by knowing your fans**: With Facebook Insights you can know where your fans are located, what kind of content they like and share. This will help you publish your content accordingly. You should also know when they are most active so that you can post during that time. There are a couple of ways to find this. One of the options on Facebook Insights is 'When Your Fans Are Online'. It also indicates how many of your fans log onto their Facebook accounts every day and how many of your fans saw your post. The only limitation is that you can see this data only for your fans and not others.

5. **Knowing which posts should be promoted:** Facebook Ads will help you budget your marketing efforts better. Facebook Ads will use a share of your marketing budget, hence it is always good to analyze for which content you should run ads and for which you shouldn't. Promoted Posts are great for marketing purposes as they increase the reach of the content you promote. Before you start allocating a budget to these ads, be sure the content is worth promoting. Ways to analyze the likelihood of success of your promoted content:

   a. Add value to the content that already exists. Analyze your existing content over a period of time to find the posts that gained good engagement.

b. Recast the content that already exists but has not been performing well. Analyze your existing content over a period of time to find posts that haven't performed well or drove little engagement. You can recast this content to give it new life.

c. Analyze the content over a period of time to find posts that have driven high engagement. Capitalize this content by running promotions around them to improve success and exposure to overall marketing strategy.

d. Analyze the content over a period of time to see what works for your competitors and industry. When you analyze your competitors to understand what they like and share, you will know the content types and topics you can promote on Facebook. Understanding what can drive good engagement and what content competitors like, can help you achieve success using an effective marketing strategy

e. Analyze the content over a period of time to find out what works on other channels. This way you can design an effective promotion plan. Measuring and evaluating this plan can help you set up effective campaigns because when you launch, you start with a better data-driven plan, saving you money and time.

6. **Knowing the impact of visual content**. The most effective form of content is the visual content, and the famous saying, "An image is worth thousand words" is true. Visuals are the most engaging type of content as

they are capable of reaching more potential customers, followers, and fans. Some of the ways to analyze your visual content to create an effective strategy are:

    a. Measure the consumptions by the post type

    b. Measure the total engagement vs. post engagement

    c. Measure engagement outside Facebook – on Instagram, Twitter etc.

7. **Dealing with negative feedback**: Your customers do not have an option to dislike your post or page but they can certainly show their frustration through negative actions, such as negative comments on your post. Because of the way the News Feed algorithm works, any negative feedback from your audience can limit your ability to reach them. Negative actions are mainly four types of negative feedback on Facebook and each of these actions comes with its own set of consequences.

    a. **Hide Clicks**: when the user clicks on a link that hides a specific post from their News Feed

    b. **Hide All Clicks**: when the user clicks to hide all the posts from a specific brand or organization from appearing on his News Feed

    c. **Page Unlikes**: When users Unlike a page

    d. **Report Spam**: When users report a post as spam

These negative feedbacks from users should be segmented to understand how it affects the reputation of a brand. For instance, when a user clicks to hide a specific post it is not as severe as it is when he chooses to hide all the posts from a brand or organization.

When someone chooses to hide all your posts, you will not be able to show them your content in the future. Therefore, analyzing all the 'Hide All Clicks' will give a clearer view of how many of your fans are restricting your content from being visible on their News Feed or are choosing not to see your posts. At the same time, analyzing the Page Unlikes can help you understand how effective you are at retaining your fans.

You can also analyze the negative feedback from your users by posts. While you are calculating the number of negative actions on your page, you can go a step further and see actions taken on specific posts. Identify the ones that got the greatest number of negative feedbacks and see the attributes that are likely to cause your fans to hide your content from appearing on their timeline, report it as spam, or Unlike it.

The Graph Search of Facebook is an amazing alternative to some of the search engines that help marketers understand how to optimize their listing to appear higher in Graph Search results. The main focus of this tool is Search Engine Optimization (SEO).

Graph Search uses certain user-driven metrics to rank the content, such as engagement on outbound content. These metrics can be analyzed to optimize the rankings.

- **Engagement on Outbound content**: People engage with the outbound content (content that you have posted on your page) just the way they engage with your posts and Stories. Now, as your focus is to get your posts, content on page and comments high in the Graph Search results, you must analyze these metrics. Facebook users certain factor to base the priority in the News Feed – one of these factors is the number of Likes you have earned from your extended network (a network of your friends). Therefore, try to pay attention to comments, stories, and content that is earning most likes and other forms of engagement.

- **Demography of Facebook Fans**: The demographic profile of your fans gives you important information about them, which can be used to design a better marketing strategy.

- **Stories on content generated by users**: Graph Search results are based on the connection users have with their friends. The Stories created by them is a key metric that increases the results. Therefore, always focus on making your content and page shareable, and create ideas that make your content appear in user's connections.

- **Using the keywords from comments**: If you focus on the important keywords that are used in the comments, it will help you do two things - create content that people are talking about and drive the search by engaging with your audience in a better way. If all the content sharing and conversations are not helping you to drive traffic to your content, design an ad campaign incorporating these keywords so that conversations are steered toward the topic you want.

It is important for the marketers to use the data Facebook provides so that they know how they are engaging with their potential customers. However, using Insights can be daunting. Identifying topics your audience is talking about is overwhelming. The good thing amidst all this is people are talking about your brand, so you just need to keep them engaged and connected by giving them what they like. Graph Search is there to help you attain this. It helps you make your job simpler by:

Searching for key terms – You can search content (posts and pages) by simply entering the key terms and you can see information that marketers can use that will reveal what their fans are saying about their companies and brands.

Searching by location – If you are running a physical store, you will be definitely interested in traffic based on the location. By entering the location, you can find information that can be used to see what people are talking about in your city and about your store, in particular.

Searching by time – You can search for posts that were posted for a specific time frame to see how your customers reacted to your business around that time. The time you are interested in might be the month or week when you ran a promotion, and therefore you want to see the response of your potential customers for that duration.

Benefits of Facebook Analytics

Something you can always count on with Facebook is new features. The aim of Facebook is to always provide something new and interesting to its users so that they always have something to explore and experiment with using. Facebook Analytics is also such a domain, and you will always find something new – a new button, a new feature, or something new that encourages you to explore it. Facebook Analytics is a comprehensive tool so the user can see the complete sales funnel, appreciate the value of users, and analyze how organic and paid strategies can be leveraged to drive best results. For all this, you need to have your own page and Pixel, and of course an active Facebook Ad account.

Facebook Pixel: The major challenge faced by most digital marketers today is <u>sales distribution</u>. Most marketers fail to understand how their data from Facebook can be intertwined with the analytic power of Google and understand the complete picture of how their ads are performing. This challenge is addressed by Facebook Pixel. If you have Pixel installed, you can easily analyze your data and understand it better. While Analytics can create tons of important data, Pixel can measure it for you. So, here are three key things you must learn about Facebook Analytics so that you know the whole story:

1. **Envisage the Sales Funnel**: Facebook ads add creativity to how you visualize your sales funnel, and Facebook Analytics makes some of the complex details available to you. With analytics, you can visualize all those who commented on your post and later added an item to their cart. You can see how many people downloaded your app and later bought something after viewing your page. Pixel integrates everything seamlessly- it helps you visualize your sales funnel better. Some of the events you should consider customizing on your site include – Add to Cart, View Content, Purchase, Lead, Initiate Checkout etc. The code for all these can be found in the Pixel installation area of your Facebook Ad account. When the code of these events is customized, you can visualize your data in a better and more effective way.

2. **Create Event Source Groups**: Fractured data is a real challenge for marketers as it gets really

complicated when you have different sources telling you different stories based on how each of these sources measures data. It is not exciting to analyze that data. The main issue due to this fractured data is there is no one common room to store the data. While Facebook tells its version of the story, we have Google Analytics telling its own version. Then we have Pixel that tracks the data. All this leads to issues and no proper connectivity. To be able to reap benefits of some of the rich features of Facebook Analytics, you should connect different assets into one Event Source Group, which is a tool available in Business Manager. You can group your apps together, your page, your Pixel, and offline event to unite the data. Once it is created, Analytics can start building charts and graphs that tell you the complete story. Since it gives you a comprehensive picture of everything you do on Facebook, it is known as the omnichannel analytics. Even if you have multiple pixels and multiple pages, you can bring it all under one Event Source Group.

3. **Illuminate and Understand Data with Visuals**: The amount of data we analyze on Facebook is overwhelming. At the same time, Facebook gives you several options to see how this data can be presented so that you can analyze it in the best possible way. Whether you are comfortable with graphs or charts, Facebook Analytics allows you to choose your own method of illustrating the data. You can customize each data point in terms of how you want to see it. Once you have selected your visual aids, these can be added on to the Analytics dashboard to have dynamic data that can be shared with clients and other people.

Facebook Delivery Insights

Another great tool on Facebook is Delivery Insights that provides additional insight into how your ads are performing. Up till now, we discussed several metrics that help us evaluate the performance of ads, but Delivery Insights give you additional information by determining the cause of any drop in performance of these ads on Facebook. It is a metric that helps understand the audience saturation. When Delivery Insights are applied to ad sets, the ads see a shift in performance.

There are three tabs that appear at the bottom of Delivery Insights – Activity History, Audience Saturation, and Auction Overlap.

Activity History is shown by default. It keeps a record all the changes that have been made to the ad set. This can help you find the cause of a drop in performance. You can analyze based on the changes you made during that time.

Auction Overlap tells you about the situation when the audience overlaps from one ad account in the same auction. Look at it this way – Facebook doesn't want you to compete against yourself. If it finds same audiences from the same ad account in multiple ad sets, the better performing ad set would be selected. Within Auction Overlap, there are three variables – Amount Spent, Auction Overlap Rate, and Overlapping Ad Set.

- Amount Spent: the amount you spend on an ad in a day. If you find that this number is dropping from the expected budget, see it as a threat that might be because of the high level of de-duping.

- <u>Auction Overlap Rate</u>: the rate at which your ad set was part of an auction that had another ad set from the same ad account. When this overlap condition is reached, the audience is deleted from the auction for the given ad set.
- <u>Overlapping Ad Set</u>: Causes your ad set to be removed from the auction due to overlap. The ad set that is causing overlap is denoted by an ID.

If you see higher percentages in the tab that displays three different overlapping ad sets, it is a problem as a higher percentage means it is causing greater overlap. Overlapping is not always bad. Suppose there are two large audiences and there is a huge overlap. If you have a low budget for your ads and if the audiences are large, it will result in two auctions competing with each other. However, if the overlap is high, there could be issues and it is recommended that the two audiences should be merged as high overlap can lead to poor performance of ads.

According to Facebook, "Here's an example scenario: After seeing an ad set targeting fans of your Page has a 50% Auction Overlap Rate, you check its Overlapping Ad Set 1. You find that it's an ad set targeting people who visited your website and that it's accounting for 60% of the auction overlap. You decide to merge the Page fans ad set into the website visitors ad set. You do this by adding the budget and targeting of the former into the latter. That way you maintain data from the successful ad set, which means it could take less time for it to adjust to the new parameters after the merge."

This shows that the problematic area is not the overlapping of the audience but the poor performance. So, if you expect your ad set to perform at a specific level but if that's not how it is and you find the auction is highly overlapping, consider merging. You can merge the ad set that is poorly performing with the one that is performing well.

Audience Saturation is the final one that appears at the bottom of Delivery Insights. It shows how many times people see your ad for the first time. The metrics that help in evaluating this are –

- Impressions: The number of times an ad (within the referred ad set) is viewed in a day.
- First time Impression Ratio: The percentage of impressions that are received by people seeing an ad from a given ad set in a day for the first time.
- Reach: The number of people who saw your ad from the referred ad set at least once during the time the campaign ran.

Delivery Insights can be really handy for advertisers who want to know what the causes of their dropping performance are. This tool can help you find the root causes and also propose a fix that you can try.

Chapter 10:

Facebook Live

It is certainly not easy to keep pace with the ever-changing features of social media platforms as they have new updates every now and then. While live video streaming is not new, Facebook Live was able to gain attention from several individuals and businesses. Facebook Live is a live video streaming feature of Facebook that was created with the intention of bringing real-life people in touch with some of the real-life characters (such as celebrities, actors, models etc.) they are interested in. With several eminent personalities and celebrities using it, it is accessible to everyone and anyone. It allows you to stream your live videos directly from a mobile without the need for additional apps. It works just like a smartphone camera that can be used to capture something live.

Since its inception, Facebook Live has been growing in popularity mainly because videos see much more engagement compared to other forms of content and millions of users around the world watch them on Facebook. Live is a fun and effective way to build relationships with the audience and communicate the brand using the power of visual media in real-time. It is a feature that brings several opportunities to connect live and enhance your sales. You can use this opportunity to tell your story your way. Marketers must know the nuances if they want to make most out of it.

Here are some of the ways you can use the Live feature for your business:

1) **Discussing a Topic:** Opening a discussion about one of your previous posts is an effective way to keep your users engaged. Even though you can reply to their comments in the post itself, it is great to have a live video session to address their queries and comments as it adds life to your content. It's as if you are talking to them in person. They can always watch this video later as it appears as any other post in their News Feed.

2) **Promote your Event**: You can have a pre-event live session and post-event follow-up session with your attendees. In the post-event session, you can also share the clickable link to them. During the event, you can share live updates for all those who couldn't be there. Give them a sneak-peek into what they are missing so that they do not miss the next opportunity.

3) **Give Updates:** If you want to give several updates about your business to your audience, Live sessions are really helpful. It is a great way to ensure they know about your business and products, and the real-time interaction boosts your relationship.

Go Live Using Mobile Devices

What started as just a broadcasting feature on mobiles became a popular broadcasting option for users of all the devices. How to "Go Live" using the mobile device:

a. Open the Facebook app on the Mobile device and log into your account. Now go to the News Feed and click on the "Live" button that is denoted by a camcorder icon. You can also go live from your profile by going to "what's on your mind" bar and then click on "Live Video"

b. You will be prompted by Facebook to give access to microphone and camera. Click "Ok"

c. Select the privacy settings depending on who you want to access your posts. If you are promoting your business, you would want your posts to be seen by everyone in this world. Hence, it should be made "public". If you are trying out a new feature and do not want anyone else to see it, you can choose the settings as "Only Me".

d. Add a description to your broadcast so that people can see it as a status update message in their News Feed. Make the description catchy so that people reading are attracted by it.

e. Add an activity, and include your location and tag your friends. You can do all this by tapping the icons that appear at the bottom of the page. You can tag the friends who are live with you in the video, add the location from where you are making the video and share what you are doing with everyone. All this will personalize your live video and increase the level of discoverability so that more and more people will want to watch the video.

f. Set the right angle for your camera. Before you go live with the video, ensure your camera is pointing in the right direction and set to the right angle by checking out the background that shows what your camera sees. To change the view of your camera, just click on the rotating arrow button that appears on top of the screen and adjust accordingly. Since the video is going to be a square, it doesn't make any difference if the camera is held vertically or horizontally. However, you can choose your image to be mirrored – horizontally or vertically, by simply tapping the magic wand icon that appears on top of the screen. Now to adjust the brightness or change the angle, just tap on tools icon at the bottom. Adjust the settings and see the magic.

g. Write on your video or add filters, drawing, or lenses by using the magic wand, which appears on top of the screen. Once you click it, it will show you options to change the filters for the camera, to add lenses to your face, and even draw something or write on the video to make it more descriptive.

h. Go Live.. Once you have adjusted all the settings and are ready to go live with your video, click on the "Go Live" button. Once you do that, the countdown will start and then your video will start broadcasting. The moment you go live, the live video will appear in the News Feed of your Facebook Page just like any other post you publish. The maximum time you can broadcast is 90 minutes. Always remember that the longer the video, the more likely it is to get noticed because if the live video goes on for long, more people will stumble upon it when they log into their Facebook accounts.

i. Respond to comments and interact with all those who are watching you live. This is one of the best and most effective ways to keep your viewers engaged – speak to them, show them what you are doing and respond to the comments they leave on your video. Do all that it takes to encourage them to watch you/your video live as it will increase your ranking in the News Feed of your connections. You can keep them engaged by talking directly to them through the video, showing them different things that might interest them or by responding to the comments from another device. You cannot use your mobile device as you would be using it to shooting the video, so use another device or have someone else to respond to their comments so that you interact with your viewers while they watch you live. When you are broadcasting, you can see various things on your screen – the time elapsed, number of people watching and the comments. But always remember that the comments appear in your feed in reverse chronological order. So, the new ones will be somewhere further down. Facebook also provides you with an option to block some of the viewers while you are broadcasting live, simply by clicking on their profile picture that appears next to the user's comments and clicking 'Block'. So, if you feel someone is commenting inappropriate things that shouldn't appear in your feed, you can block that viewer any time you want. Later you can unblock someone if you wish to.

j. Once you are done, click on 'Finish' to end the live video. Once you end it, the video will appear on the timeline as just another post or video.

k. Save your video to your mobile device once you finish the broadcast by clicking on the download button that appears on the screen.

l. You can change the settings of the video by going back to the timeline and selecting the video that appears as a post. The same way you edit any other post in your timeline, you can edit the settings for this video. Click on the privacy settings and you will be given options to Save Video, Edit it, Edit the privacy, Delete, or Turn off the notification for it.

That's it! It is simple to Go Live. You can also broadcast a live video using your desktop device if you are an editor of your Facebook Page. Although it won't be as spontaneous as it is from a mobile device, it can be used while filming static videos.

You shot a live video and went live, and you also posted it on your timeline after it was finished. But this is not enough. It is also important to analyze the performance of your live video to see how effective it was in engaging people and how people liked it. For this, you need to know how to access the video analytics on a Business Page.

Accessing Video Analytics

To get started, look for the Insights tab on the top of your Facebook Business Page to analyze the Live Broadcasts on Facebook.

Now browse through the left-hand side of the screen and look for the 'Videos' option on the menu. Click on it and look for 'Top Videos' section within the Videos, and choose from the options given. You can either choose any one of the videos from the list displayed or look for all the videos you have posted on your page by clicking on 'Video Library'.

The analytics related to performance for Live videos are quite similar to those of any other video that appears on Facebook, along with certain additional features. For normal videos, Facebook allows you to analyze features, such as unique viewers, video views, average percentage completion, comments, shares, reactions from viewers, and minutes viewed. For Live Videos, Facebook gives you an option to analyze all the listed metrics plus additional metrics –

average watch time, peak live viewers, people reached, demographics of viewers who watched the live video, and average watch time. As well as these metrics, you can see how each of the metrics changed over a period of time when the video went live. You can do this by selecting the metric that you want to track. You can also see the profile information of each of the viewers who were watching your video live. Now that we know how to track the metrics and analyze the performance of the video, here are some tips and tricks to get the most out of these live videos.

Tips and Tricks to Get the Most out of your Live Videos

If you get into the nuances of it, you would know that there are several little things that you can do to get the most out of these live videos on Facebook. For example, a video from a brand was shot in five different parts and in different cities across the globe and showcases how a woman can make changes to her life. This five-part video was later analyzed for its performance and a couple of things became clear.

1) Always test the live video first by shooting it in 'Only Me' mode. This way the live video will be visible only to you and will appear only in your timeline.
2) The Live videos should be spaced properly with other posts that appear in the timeline. Facebook Live Videos rank higher than any other post or video that appears in your timeline, and therefore, it is recommended that these live videos should be spaced well with other posts and content so that you can

maximize the organic reach of your content on Facebook.

3) Always introduce yourself, even if you are creating a multi-series video and even though it is not the first time you are shooting a video. Talk about what the video is about to create a background for what the viewers are going to watch over next few minutes. Remember that when you start streaming, you might not have anybody watching you but you might have viewers after a few seconds or minutes. Hence, reintroduce yourself again so new viewers can catch up. In our example, when the video is being shot in each of the cities, he reintroduces himself. Don't worry. You can always make it sound engaging and interesting:

"Hello, Friends! Lindi here! I don't know if anyone has joined yet, so I am going to wait for a few seconds to see who joins us".

And then after 30-40 secs: "Hello friends, welcome to The Women's Challenge. You are with Lindi and just to tell you what's happening now, this is Episode One of our new initiative 'The Women's Challenge'."

In this manner, you can reintroduce yourself 2-3 times so that all the new joiners know who you are and the motive behind shooting the video.

4) Make your video as interesting as possible. Visuals have to be really engaging – not just in the beginning but throughout the video so that more and more people join you when they stumble upon it. The more engaging you make it, the easier it will be for you to make the viewers stay with you through the shot.

Keep your camera rolling and keep up your energy level because if you yourself are not interested, you can never make it engaging for your viewers. Move around as much as you can and show them what you are doing. This way you not only get more viewers but also get higher rank in the News Feeds of your connections. If you don't know, Facebook monitors the signs of engagement when people enable high definition, turn on their audio, and switch to fullscreen mode. All these are the signs that people are watching your video and find it engaging. Due to this reason, the News Feed algorithm has been tweaked in a way that more engaging videos appear higher in the feed.

5) Do not worry about stutters or mistakes as 'to err is human'. We all make mistakes and something that is spontaneous is prone to errors. When you are making a live video, things might not turn out the way you had expected, and this could be due to technical difficulties or human errors. You might lose words, your equipment might malfunction, you could lose your thoughts, or you might be photobombed by some unwanted person or animal. When any of these things happen, you can rollback or say "cut" and retake. You have to live with it and keep going. After all, you are Live. But never worry about these things as all this adds an element of reality to your videos. Live videos are rarely flawless. So, just deal with the issues. If you lose your words, you make it a joke. If you are photobombed, make that person a part of your video. If your phone trembles, laugh it off. The important thing is to keep going despite all the distractions that come along your way. Keep it light so the

communication will continue with your viewers. There is always a way to cover up mistakes.

6) Ensure the video is spontaneous as that what makes a Live Video live – they are interactive, they are spontaneous. People love the originality of content and respect that you are not trying to build anything; they really like the interaction, the novelty of what you are trying to show them, and the reality of the moment you are shooting. The viewers should feel they are a part of that scene when they view it. All these elements make the live video real and special, and that's what distinguishes them from edited, scripted pre-recorded videos.

7) Call out your viewers to share and like your Live Video. As we discussed, one of the ways the News Feed algorithm uses to rank content is the number of times it has been shared or liked. The more people like and share your broadcasted video, the higher it will be seen on the News Feed of your connections. So, encourage your viewers to share it in their network. When a viewer is watching a video, he gets distracted from sharing or liking as compared to when he is reading a post. Facebook knows this and that's why they started monitoring different types of engagement signals around the videos, such as turning on the audio.

Here's how you can ask your viewers to share and like the video:

- If you guys like this broadcast, be a part of it and also share it with your friends.
- Share this video with your girlfriend who thinks she is independent and brave.

- Thank you guys for liking my video. I can see my screen has turned blue because of all the thumbs up I am getting from you.
- At least one thumb up if you like me.

8) Interact with those who comment on your video, and if possible address them by name. Getting comments is another way to get a higher score so that there are more chances it shows up in News Feed of your friends. Encourage them to leave their comments and respond to those who are commenting to keep the communication line open. If someone asks a question, do not lose any opportunity to answer them and address them by name. This not only gets you more viewers but also creates a fun, interactive experience for all the viewers so that they stay with you longer.

9) Include a subtitle for your video in the comment section so that people know what you are talking about. People cannot be online all the time and viewers tune in and out of the video during their work hours, and some of them might watch it without sound. It is always good to subtitle the broadcast in the comments section so that all those who cannot turn on the sound or watch it continuously, can read the subtitles to catch up on what's going on. This is a brilliant way to keep your viewers engaged.

10) Have someone read the comments from your viewers and respond to them from another device. It is really difficult to see the comments that pop up on your mobile that you are holding to shoot a live video. If these comments pop up fast, you are likely to lose sight of them as they disappear when the new ones come in. Also, it is not a good idea to focus on these comments as you might get distracted in shooting

your video. Since you are live, you should focus only on recording and engaging with your viewers. Due to this, have someone help you with these comments. Have a dedicated person who can log in from another device and read the comments from your viewers. This way, they can read and respond to your viewers and keep the engagement ongoing, to create a great interactive experience.

11) Always aim to broadcast for at least 10 minutes so that more and more people view it. When you start, you might not have many viewers for your live broadcast, but as your video starts showing up in the News Feeds of people, they will start viewing it. Therefore, the longer you broadcast, the greater the chances that people will discover your video and act on it. Some of them might like it, some will comment and others might share it with their friends. Timing plays a key role in video engagement and that's why it is recommended that you should go live for at least 10 minutes, if not more. However, the maximum time you can stay live is 90 minutes.

12) Call out to your viewers to subscribe to live notifications. Besides asking your viewers to like, comment and share your video, you can encourage them to subscribe to live notifications. To do this, the viewers just have to do a small thing – they just have to click on a downward facing arrow that is located at the top of the screen and then select "Turn On Notifications". You can also invite them to like your organization or brand so that they get notified of the updates to the next live videos.

13) Always end your video with an engaging line that compels your viewers to wait for the next update from you. You can also finish your broadcast by saying

something like "I will be going live again soon so watch this space for more details", or "If you want to know the answers to all the questions, follow me and watch out my next video".

14) Add a trackable link to the description of your broadcast so that your viewers can be directed to the page where you will be publishing the next series of your videos. Once the broadcast is over, the video appears in the timeline like just any other post and can be edited or deleted. Once the broadcast is over, you can go back and include a clickable link to the post description so that the future viewers can be easily directed to your video series page. To be able to edit the description, just click on downward facing arrow on the post and select 'Edit post' and make the changes.

Benefits to Marketers of Going Live

The increased use of mobile devices and the growing popularity of social media channels have ensured the potential of videos posted on social media reaches the position as the monarch of content. Today, people are creating and watching videos like never before, and these videos are highly engaging. Amidst all this, Facebook has added life with its Facebook Live Videos. These videos benefit marketers by:

- Facebook Live videos help drive more engagement. People comment ten times more on these live videos than to the normal videos and they spend more time watching these live videos than pre-recorded ones.

- Facebook Live videos offer amazing real-time experience to the users.
- They boost the organic reach of the marketers.
- Live videos are considered as a different form of content on Facebook, and even the News Feed algorithm considers them as separate entities. This is the main reason why Live videos tend to appear higher in the timelines.
- The Live videos also come with a notification service. When someone in your network goes live, you will be notified about it. This gives the marketers an edge and prominence and keeps them in the minds of users.

Features Offered by Facebook Live Videos

Facebook Live Videos not only give immense brand access to the users but also boost the interactivity with its amazing set of features.

Notification Service: Facebook Live Videos are considered a distinct content type that has its own notification service. This notification service is set to be On by default. Therefore, when someone goes live, people who recently interacted or were frequently engaged with that person will receive a notification. If someone is interested in watching live videos from a particular brand or organization, he can subscribe to the live video notification from that brand so that he can receive notification whenever they go live.

Send Invitation to Friends: When a viewer is watching a live video, he has an option to send an invitation to a friend to watch the video. This option is available to him from the Live Video itself. He can just tap the invite icon on the screen and select the friend that he wants to invite, and the invitation will be sent to that person.

Live Maps: If you are interested in discovering something new, Facebook Live Videos presents Live Maps, which can be viewed from the desktop site. Using the map feature, you can see all the live videos that are being broadcast in different parts of the world, each represented with a blue dot on the map. If you are interested in knowing about the famous live broadcasts happening around the world, you can look for the bigger dots on the live map. You can also get a sneak-peek into the live video by hovering your mouse over these dots. This also provides information, such as how long the video has been playing, how many people are watching the live streaming at the moment and so on. When you zoom in the map, you can look for broadcasts in specific regions. You can also see a list of all the popular broadcasts happening in the world by checking the panel on the left side of the screen.

Live Reactions: Facebook users can express themselves and react to the posts using the emotions given by the platform. Users have been given six emoji to highlight their responses. with Facebook Live, viewers can react to the video stream in real-time using the reactions that appear on their screens at the time of the broadcast. They can click on any of these to express an opinion.

Filters: With Facebook Live, marketers have an option to add filters to the live video stream. You just have to click on the magic wand icon that appears on the screen and then scroll left to explore other options. Once you find a suitable option, click on it to add the filter.

Masks: Facebook users can now explore the option of Snapchat-Like masks at the time of broadcasting their video. All you need to do is to click on the Live video icon that appears on the screen to start recording. Then click on the magic wand to apply masks. Select the mask from the creative tools that appear at the bottom of the screen. Browse through the given options and click on the mask that you want to apply. Once you click it, it will automatically appear on the video. If you do not like the mask, you can always remove it by selecting the "no mask" option by scrolling the bar at the left.

When is it best to use Facebook Live

You can use the power of Facebook Live Videos anytime you wish, but some of the best ways to use live videos are:

1) **Hot topics** – When there is something that is on everyone's mind, it is good to talk and discuss it. Consider having a real-time conversation with your audience using Live broadcasting. Always bear in mind that you should have these conversations only when you have something useful and relevant to say.

2) **Questions and Answers** – Knowing the need of Questions and Answers, Facebook Live has been creative with interactivity. Hence, users can easily interact with the host and ask their questions about the topic of discussion. These questions can be asked in comments in real-time.

3) **Live events and performances** – Facebook Live is a good platform to host live events whether it is about a live performance or conference. As these live sessions are available to a broader audience, it broadens the scope of your event. Create live videos whenever you want to reach a larger audience, before the event, during the event, and after the event.

4) **Important News** – If you are into media, Facebook Live is a perfect platform for you to broadcast breaking news. However, if you are on Facebook to promote your brand or organization that is not into media, things are slightly different. In such cases, probably you can talk about something important that your organization has done and you want people to know about it.

5) **Behind-the-scenes content** – Many social channels are popular to talk about behind-the-scenes content, especially video channels. Facebook Live gives you an edge over these channels by providing you the ability to interact with your audience and ask questions in real-time.

You can use also use Facebook Live for a lot of other things, such as demos, advertisement campaigns, live sessions, series, announcements and so on.

Chapter 11:

Facebook Pixel for Advertisers

Facebook Pixel is one of the important tools for tracking ad results. Facebook Pixel is generally used by advanced advertisers who want to gain better insight into their campaign results.

Facebook Pixel helps you to –

➤ Ensure your Facebook ads are bringing in results. Once you have installed Facebook Pixel on your website, you can easily track the conversions brought in by your Facebook Ad Campaign. There are different types of conversions, but you can use either Custom or Standard events, such as purchase completions, installation of apps etc.

➤ Create an advanced ads audience. If you want to create ads that effectively reach your target audience, you should use advanced audience: Lookalike audience and Custom audience

➤ Learn about various other Facebook advertising tools and metrics. Facebook Pixel allows you to set up new types of conversions that drive enrichment for the reports that you can see in the Ads Manager. You can also use additional setup campaigns and bidding methods if you want to have more conversions through your mobile app or website

Installation of Facebook Pixel

Installing and setting up Pixel is quite simple and quick. First, ensure you do not have any pixels installed by navigating to Facebook Business Manager and find the Pixel section. Once you are sure you haven't installed it, click on 'Create a Facebook Pixel' button. This will take you to a new pop-up window where you will be asked to enter the Pixel name and click on the Next button. Next, install the Pixel code on your website by using either of the two options given – use a Facebook integrator or Google Tag manager, or copy and paste the Pixel code to your website. It is always simple to just copy and paste the Pixel code that appears at the bottom of the header section of your website right above the head tag. Ensure this code is copied onto each web page or use a template to have it on the entire website so that it is available on all the pages.

Apart from tracking the visitors on your website, Pixel also helps you track nine different Standard events –

- ➤ View content
- ➤ Search
- ➤ Add to cart
- ➤ Add to wishlist
- ➤ Initiate checkout
- ➤ Add payment info
- ➤ Make purchase
- ➤ Lead
- ➤ Complete registration

Define the Conversions

If you chose the Standard events as an option to track your ad campaign results, the good news is that Standard events are already measured by Facebook conversions. If you are using custom events or if you want to use URL based rules, you might have to take some additional steps.

- Go to Ads Manager and navigate to Facebook Pixel tab.
- Click on Create Conversion and select Track Custom Conversions.
- You will be asked to enter 'Rule' that includes traffic that meets the given conditions. From the drop-down menu, select Standard Event. If the event is accompanied with parameters, you can select the key pair value here.
- For 'category', from the drop-down menu select the option that best fits your requirements.
- Name the custom conversion.

That's it – you have set up your Pixel and now you can start seeing the data. This Pixel page can be accessed from the primary menu of Business Manager. The Pixel page will highlight:

- <u>Time Frame</u> – you can adjust the time frame for conversion tracking.
- <u>Toolbar</u> – you can set up Pixel- based audiences and Create Ad campaigns. You can edit the Pixel's name under Actions, and you can also view your Pixel code and share it using Business Manager.

- <u>Traffic data</u> – you can see how much traffic is there on your website. When you do not see a firm line but a dotted line, it means the data is not yet published.
- <u>Facebook pixel details</u> – you see the basic information about your Pixel – status, last activity and so on.
- <u>Custom Audience</u> – you can see the Custom Audiences using Pixel.
- <u>Data Filters</u> – you can break down your data based on domain, URL, events and see how much traffic is displayed for each of these filters.

Chapter 12:

Advertising on Instagram: Facebook's Marketing Partner

Facebook now offers you another brilliant way to advertise your brand or products – Instagram, the art gallery. Since 2010, Instagram is an integrated part of Facebook and as Facebook is already doing some big things in advertising, the same structure offers the best advertising experience with Instagram too. This means Facebook advertisers can use all the audience and targeting options that they have been using on Facebook – Demographic, Custom Audience, Open targeting and so on. Users come to this platform to express themselves and be inspired to take actions on posts. It is a serious advertising platform for you to share your stories with your audience in fun way. So, if you are a Facebook advertiser, you can now select these stories as a placement to run your creative ads. However, you will not be able to select the Instagram Story your ad will be featured on or in, just the way you can't select the website or video for your ads.

Advertise on Instagram: If you want to know what will attract the audience available on Instagram, it is good to first know about the behavior of users of Instagram (the same way you learned about your audience on Facebook). Know what they are looking for when they log into their Instagram account. According to studies conducted, more than 60% of the users use this platform to see videos and images that inspire them. The rest use it to share updates with their connections. This is important information as the majority of

Instagram users access it to get inspired, and that's what makes it different from other platforms. Therefore, if your ad objectives are to inspire, you must use it to advertise your business.

Creating Instagram Ads

Being a Facebook advertiser, it would be quite easy for you to set up your ads on Instagram as the steps are quite similar. Since the two platforms are merged, even though you want to create ads on Instagram, most of the steps are taken care of Facebook – setup, scheduling, budgeting etc.

To be able to use Instagram for your advertising goals, the first thing is to connect your Instagram account to your ad account on Facebook. To do this:

- Log into your Business Manager account and then go to the Settings.
- Navigate to 'People and Assets' and then click on 'Instagram Accounts'.
- Once you click this, you will be shown a tab 'Claim New Instagram Account', click on it.
- Enter your Instagram login details. This should be the ad account that you want to use to access Instagram.

Once you log in, follow these steps to create ads:

Step 1: Create your ad campaign

Instagram ads can be created using Ads Manager, Facebook Ads API, or Power Editor. Select one of the tools based on how many ads you want to use. If you intend to manage large campaigns, you might want to use the Power Editor. However, Ads Manager is something that any advertiser can use. Once you select an editor, you can choose to either create a new campaign or view the existing campaigns. If you are just starting with Instagram advertising, you can start by creating a new campaign.

Step 2: Select your ad objective

Just like Facebook, Instagram gives you options to choose from a list of ad objectives:

- Boost your post
- Increase conversions on your website
- Divert traffic to your website
- Get people to install your app
- Increase engagement
- Get Video views

For now, select traffic as our ad objective. Once selected, you will be prompted to add a name to your campaign. Although you can give any name to it, it is an opportunity for you to enhance your brand awareness. So, choose the name appropriately.

Step 3: Choose your target audience

If you are just starting out on Instagram, you might not know much about your target audience. So, choose the same audience as you have on Facebook. You can choose from these options:

- Location
- Age
- Gender

- Language
- Relationship
- Education
- Work
- Financial Status
- Home
- Parents
- Ethnic Affinity
- Life Events
- Interests
- Behavior
- Connections

You can also create a Custom Audience to reach out to those with whom you have already interacted, for your business, or a Lookalike Audience to target the people on Facebook who have similar interests as your potential customers. You can also save the audience set you just created so that you can use it again sometime in the future.

Since your ad objective is to get more traffic on our website, you need to be more specific while targeting so that more relevant people hit your website. To achieve this, navigate to 'Detailed Targeting' option and apply filters such as interests, behavior or demographics to have a more targeted audience. Facebook also provides a definition gage to give you a feel of the audience you are targeting – narrow or broad, and a roughly estimated reach of your ad. Since, for this example, not too many filters and definitions have been added; it appears to be broad.

Step 4: Choose the placement for your ad

This is the distinguishing feature – the biggest one. If you want to go ahead with the Instagram ad, you must unselect all the options leaving 'Instagram'.

Step 5: Set your budget and schedule

For your ads, you can either choose daily budget or lifetime budget. If you choose to set it as a daily budget, your ads will run continuously throughout the day, which means the algorithm will drive your budget through the day. Also, there is a minimum limit that you can set for your daily budget, based on certain factors. If you want to choose lifetime budget, your ad will run for a specific time period, which means the algorithm will drive the budget through the defined time frame.

Another thing to deal with is setting the schedule for your campaign. You need to select when you want the campaign to start and when it should stop. There are also options for you to set your campaign to run only during certain hours of the day.

Next – you need to optimize your campaign for ad delivery, which means you can set parameters that impact who can see your ad. To do this, you have three options – Link Clicks, Impressions, or Daily Unique Reach. Link Clicks is the recommended option, delivers your ads in a way that you get the maximum number of clicks to your website by spending least amount of money. This is driven by the algorithm the platform uses. If you choose Impressions, your ads will be delivered to your target audience a maximum number of times. If you see the same ad in your feed, again and again, it means the advertiser has chosen this method. With Daily Unique Reach, the ad will be shown to people once a day. They might see it multiple times, but not on the same day.

Now, you need to set the bid amount, which evaluates how effectively the ad is shown to your target audience. You might find you are competing with some other advertisers who might be targeting the same set of audience. You need to set up the bid amount accordingly so that you do not lose in the game. You have two options to achieve this – manual or automatic. With manual setting, you can set a price for your link clicks. If you are trying to achieve a lot with link clicks, it is recommended that you set a bid higher than the suggested value so that your ad is shown over another advertiser who has set a lower bid amount. With automatic settings, it is completely left up to the algorithm to deliver your ad, and ideally, it should get you the most number of clicks with the lower cost. You can also set the bid amount based on impressions if not link clicks.

Now, it's time to set the schedule for the delivery of your ads. To do this, you have two options – Standard and Accelerated. While Standard shows your ads the entire day, Accelerated helps you reach your target audience for time-sensitive ads in lesser time. A point that should be noted here is if you chose the 'Accelerated' option, you will have to opt for manual bid pricing.

Step 6: Select the ad creative

First, choose the format you want for your ad. You can apply your creativity here as you can decide how you want your ad to look, and of course it should resonate with the theme of your ad objective. Instagram gives you four options for your ad format – single image, carousel, slideshow, or video. Once you select an ad format, upload the visual – image or video, depending on what you have selected. However, you must keep in mind specifications for each type of format and ensure you adhere to it.

Formats and specifications (Ref: Instagram)

File Type

- .jpeg
- .png

Text/Caption

- Recommended: 125 characters
- Maximum: 2,200 characters

For Square of Video Instagram Ads

- Recommended Image Size: 1080 x 1080 pixels
- Minimum Resolution Accepted: 600 x 600 pixels
- Image Aspect Ratio: 1:1

For Landscape Image or Video Instagram Ads

- Recommended Image Size: 1200 x 628 pixels
- Minimum Resolution Accepted: 600 x 600 pixels
- Image Aspect Ratio: 1:1

Step 7: Select your page and link

Once you have set all other things, it is time to connect your Facebook Page to your Instagram account. Select the Business Page of the account that you want to use to run the ads on Instagram. If you have already logged into Instagram using your Facebook ads account, you can skip this step.

Since you are looking to run ads on Instagram, you also need to connect your Instagram account to your ad account on Facebook. To achieve this, tap on 'Add Account' using your Instagram credentials. Even if you do not have an Instagram account, you can still run your ads on it - the ads will now come from your Facebook Business Page. In simple words, your Facebook profile and page name will be used to address your business in your ad on Instagram.

Once you add the page, the next step is to include your website URL. This is a very crucial step as including your URL will help you drive more traffic – which is your ad objective.

Add a meaningful and catchy headline. This is another opportunity for you to reach out to your target audience as this headline is something that will not only be visible to the viewers of your Instagram ads but others too. Hence, if it is search engine optimized, it will reach more people.

Add a caption for your campaign, ensuring it is not more than the defined limit of 2200 characters.

Include a Call-to-action based on what the page you will have for your audience. You can either include a button that they can click, or have any of these:

- Watch more
- Book more
- Learn more
- Apply now
- Contact us
- Sign up
- Download now
- Hope now

Since your ad objective is to drive more traffic to our website, you can use 'Learn More'.

Step 8: Order by clicking on 'Place Order' button. Before you click on it, ensure you check everything.

Step 9: Watch how you are performing. Your ad is now up and running, but the job is not fully done. You need to keep an eye on your ads to see how you are performing on Instagram. You can always go back and adjust the settings if you feel you should make changes to perform better. Results of the ads can be seen in two places – Facebook Ads Manager and Marketing software.

- Facebook Ads Manager: Facebook Ads Manager offers a sophisticated view of all the campaigns, and you can see data on reach, the amount spent, and cost per result for your campaign. You can also customize the settings to see specific data. Click on the button that says "Columns: Performance" on the upper right-hand corner of the screen and then click on the drop-down menu. You will see an option to customize the columns so choose the columns you want to see for measuring the performance of your campaign. You can select columns like 'Add to Cart', CPC etc.

- Marketing software: When there are so many metrics that can be tracked, it is easy to lose focus. That's why you have an option to use marketing software to measure the full-funnel effectiveness of your ads. By tracking the specific codes in the marketing software, you can see how many customers or leads you could gain with the help of Instagram advertising campaign. This information will help you measure your ROI to see the worth of your campaigns on the platform. There are several types of marketing software available for this purpose in the market today, so choose one that best suits your requirements.

Use Instagram

Instagram is awesome; it is fun, easy, and effective. You are a new travel blogger and you can use all the visibility you can get. Well, fret not because outside of Facebook and Twitter, there is another more popular account known as Instagram.

In a world of social networking, the number of followers, likes, and shares are the indicators of success. Instagram is simple, fair and 'square' and really successful. The passionate users are the real strength of this community. Imagine your visibility if you were to get even $1/4^{th}$ of the community's attention!

However, the problem is that there is no formula that can assure you popularity on Instagram. You can develop a large following and feel like an instant-celebrity. It may be slow, frustrating even, but it is possible to pass these barriers and become an Instagram rockstar. Your reasons can be anything, from personal gratification to building a brand. It doesn't matter what drives your motivation, but it is tempting to see the numbers surge and to have some real people follow your life closely. The only mantra to successful growth in Instagram ranks is honesty with your users and not use trickery to increase followers. Don't fixate on numbers because you need a lot more than just plain followers, you need user engagement!

If you signed into Instagram only recently, here are some steps to help you reach the zenith of followership and popularity.

Find Your Niche

Before anything else, you need to know what your Instagram

account stands for. You need to have consistency of theme, passion, and niche in your account. If you are a photographer, you should only post photos that showcase your talent. Your followers follow you because of your quality work and not because of the occasional sandwich you grab with your friends! There are all kinds of people doing all kinds of things on Instagram. However, in all the popular accounts, the only common objective is that they all have a focus area and everything they post about is associated with that niche.

Make Your Account Look Attractive

You can catch more flies with honey than with vinegar, an old saying but a powerful one. If you want to attract people to your account, make it attractive and make it look inviting. Do whatever it takes to make your account look great. A cool profile and a good description is the starting point. Your photo feed has to look great because ultimately that is what will keep the followers coming and the ones you already have, interested. Build a portfolio that includes 20 high-quality images focused on your account's niche. Remove all the photos that are ugly and irrelevant.

Before people click the Follow button, it is common for them to review your account and see if they want these images to pop on their feed or not. If the photos that you post are boring, silly, and uninteresting, then don't be surprised if you fail to create any buzz.

Take Advantage of your Other Social Media Profiles

The best place to get started after creating a good-looking

Instagram profile is the existing channels and platforms. You can get a direct link to your Instagram profile if you go to Instagram.com/username. You can post this link to your Twitter, Facebook and other profiles for the people to follow you from other platforms. You can also quickly sift through your email account and send a short email to all your contacts telling them about your presence on Instagram. By these efforts alone you can get an upwards of 100 likes/follows if you have a good social media network.

Connect With Other Instagram Users

You have exhausted the list of people from your own networks, now is the time to venture out and connect with people who might be interested in the kind of photos you post. The best way to get the attention of someone on Instagram is by leaving a pleasant or complimentary comment on their posts. This will entice the account holder to check out your profile and follow you if your profile looks interesting to them. You can write what you like about the photo or leave a comment about their artistic sense in capturing the frame. However, don't do anything you don't genuinely feel. Only leave a comment if you think that the picture warranted it. Your intent will show in your comment.

Refrain from using any spammy techniques that people use to gain followers on Instagram. This method will not get you the kind of followers you want for your profile. These people are only looking for someone to follow and will soon unfollow you. You need people you can engage with and build an actual community based on these people.

Never Underestimate the Power of User Engagement

You need to engage with your followers. Don't just keep posting anything and everything. Quality trumps quantity every day. To have quality engagement with the followers and other Instagram users, you do not post multiple photos at once. Give it at least 6 hours between posts. Too many photos will only annoy the users and will make them unfollow you at once.

Most importantly, when your followers leave comments and start a discussion, make sure that you participate, even if it is a simple thank you. This is a good strategy to acknowledge the people who take the time to write you a comment.

Never Set your Profile to Private

Unless your profile is meant only for your friends and family members, never set it to private. It is discouraging for a follower to go through an approval process and would rather not follow you to avoid the hassle. Public account is a must if you need as many followers as possible. However, if you are worried about the privacy of your account, it is better to not post anything that you will regret later. To stay safe online, avoid sharing personal information.

Follow Many People on Instagram

This is the easiest and one of the most effective ways to reach out to the people and gain more followers in the process. You need to get out of your rabbit hole and reach out to the Instagram community. Start with following lots of accounts that you can unfollow later if you think they are irrelevant.

Follow all the accounts that are associated with what you do. If you get new followers, always follow them back as a gesture.

Time Your Instagram Posts

According to research, the best time to post something on Instagram is after 5 PM on Wednesday. You will get more attention if your content is posted at a time when the people are most likely to look at their feed. This is why you need to avoid posting between 8 am and 5 pm. The best time to post is early morning or late evenings to get maximum visibility.

Add Captions to Your Pictures

Out of context pictures are rarely exciting even if you clicked a good shot. You can add witty lines, a joke, or something exciting that can gain the attention of the followers. You can also use ironic captions to highlight your pictures. A combination of hashtags, emoji, and text will make a good caption.

Only Use Relevant Hashtags

Hashtags are the best ways to promote your picture to people who don't follow you. Your posts will show up when the people search hashtags related to particular themes. Using accurate hashtags and the trending ones can reveal your posts to a whole new set of people. Only use the tags that are accurate and relevant to your post. You can even add the location to your pictures through the Geotag feature. Researchers say that 11 hashtags are optimal for a post. Anything more will look desperate and less could cost you precious followers.

If Someone Likes Your Pictures, Follow Them Back

It is a good gesture to connect with people who reach out to you. You can also engage more by commenting on one of their pictures and liking a few from their profile. This small effort will help build a relationship with your follower.

Study the Trends

Check out popular hashtags and see what is trending in the Instagram community. The simplest hashtag such as #budgettravel will give you lots of options. Take your time and view the posts. Like the images you think are genuinely good and feel free to drop a line or two to the account holder. You can also check their activity tab to see what kind of pictures they post and what is currently popular.

Be a Story Teller

Your Instagram is not just a way to attract followers; it is a way to share your creative life through pictures. You can also combine stories with these images and make things more interesting. Use anything from a witty line to an interesting snippet about the image. The trick is to stay with the theme but still be diverse. You can combine these pictures together and make a pictorial story. Be creative with your posts and find ways to attract people to your profile.

Only Post Content That Is Clean

To post abusive, violent, or sexual content is violating the network's terms and conditions and you risk having your account canceled. To become popular on Instagram means that you need to keep your content worthy of sharing and to be viewed by people of all ages/PG-13 at most. Do not use cheap tactics of vulgarity or another such type of content to attract followers to your account. Not all publicity is good publicity. By using such means, you will be defeating the whole purpose of using Instagram and the reason why you want to be popular in the first place.

Exploit the Filter Functionality

Filters on Instagram have been added for a reason and you can use these options on your pictures to enhance their colors, beauty, and aestheticism. When you use them judiciously, it automatically attracts more followers and likes on your pictures. You can also use the popular tag "#nofilter" if you did not add a filter to your image. The whole point of a filter is to make a boring picture look more exciting.

Chapter 13:

Common Facebook Advertising Mistakes and Solutions

There is no doubt today, Facebook is one of the most powerful and robust advertising platforms that can be used by businesses of all types and sizes to reach their target customers. Yes, there is a lot of trial and error involved in the beginning until you get acquainted and experienced with this platform and its capabilities. If Facebook has not resulted in enough sales or you are not able to see the expected returns on the investment you made on Facebook ads, you need to look at some of the common mistakes most advertisers make and the ways to make corrections efficiently.

Mistake 1: Not investing enough time and money in audience research

Targeting is the most important part of good advertising on Facebook. Facebook is the home to various kinds of audiences and based on your ad objective, you should select the size and type of your audience. You might have to experiment in the beginning before you start seeing the actual results, but it doesn't mean you can't start the process with educated guesses. The best way to determine if you are targeting the right audience is to put yourself in their shoes and ask yourself if you would want to spend your dollars to buy the product listed. You need to find the niche that resonates with your product or brand. So, put yourself in their shoes and ask yourself:

- What will you look for?
- What kind of pages would you like on Facebook?
- What kind of apps would you like to use?
- What kind of content would you read?
- What kind of people will you follow?

Do some research and find out about their interests and problems. If you can offer a solution to their issues, it will build trust in you.

Another way of doing this is to find a page that relates to research you have done about your target audience and add it to your profile. Facebook will then show you related pages that can offer you similar interests.

Mistake 2: Targeting an audience that is too large and broad

One of the most common mistakes advertisers make while running a paid ad campaign on Facebook is they target a broad audience thinking the ad should reach as many people as possible. This isn't the right way of promoting your brand. Since it is a paid campaign, you are paying for the reach of your ad, so don't pay to make the ad reach those who are not even interested. Smaller but the right target audience is effective in driving results. If your audience is too broad, try to narrow it based on their actions and interests.

Mistake 3: Advertisers lose patience

When advertisers run paid campaigns and do not see results flowing in, most of them lose patience and this is one of the biggest mistakes. Out of this impatience, they become overwhelmed and tweak the ads to optimize them to see some real results. They must understand that patience is the key. Gathering data and insight takes time and all this must be done correctly since these are essential elements of good advertising. It is important to give your ads some time and not to tweak them until you at least reach out to people. Once you reach out to enough people, you will build enough data to analyze the performance of your ads on Facebook. Driving sales is not important in the beginning – the focus should be to reach as many people as possible so that you learn their behavior.

Mistake 4: Not testing one variable at a time

Insights are often underestimated in the world of advertising in the quest to see results. While it is always recommended that advertisers should experiment and test the ads, they can only learn the details when one variable is tested at a time. Testing data from different sources that are exposed to different ads for different time frames is not going to produce important results. You might see some positive numbers but you don't know what drove those results – the sources, the time frame, or the quality of the ad. It can even be the combination of these attributes. Isolate the variables as much as you can and test them individually to understand what's bringing you good results and what's not. Also, bear in mind that you can test at different levels in the Ad Manager account and below are the variables you can use at each of these levels:

- Ad Campaign: the objective Facebook optimizes – purchases, Add to Cart etc.
- Ad Set: your ad placement, targeting, scheduling etc.
- Ads: the format of the ads, links etc.

Mistake 5: Not properly utilizing the amount spent on the ads

Most advertisers have their ad objective as driving sales, but it is important to understand that you can expect a lot of other things from your ad. Sales are not the only possible return you should look forward to. Even from the ads that failed to produce returns, you can learn lot of things about your potential customers, such as – their email address, getting more Likes and Comments on the posts you share with them, retargeting all those who showed interest in your brand but didn't convert, interacting directly with those who commented on your ads, inviting all those who liked and commented on your ads to like your Facebook Page. There is a lot of valuable information you can derive from these ads, so utilize each and every bit of it. It is recommended that you set up Google Analytics and other analytics tools to analyze and track the performance of your ads. This will also help you understand the problems of your customers and perhaps you can provide a solution to their issues.

Mistake 6: Not optimizing your ad to get more clicks and engagement

Once you know you are targeting the right set of audiences, you can create catchy ads to help you see better and more improved results. Some of the things to make your ads look attractive are:

- Collecting social proof such as likes, comments, and shares every time the ad is run as this helps you reach your audience more effectively.
- Focusing on elements that gain the attention of the customers.
- Experimenting with different types of ad formats.
- Creating multiple click-through opportunities using tags and links.

Mistake 7: Not reaping benefits from available insights

Facebook Insights offers many features but most of these are lost due to their complexity, especially when it is about determining the performance of your ads to gather insights. For example, if you look at the defaults columns that are displayed in the Ads Manager, they do not show all the data that is available and could come in handy to you. Therefore, you must customize this selection of columns to get what you want. If not checked, see if the columns listed below are selected as they give you a good overview of your performance:

- **CTR: the Click-Through-Rate** - The percentage of people who made an attempt to click your ad after seeing it.
- **Cost-per-click**: The amount that you are paying for each click on your Facebook Ad.
- **Website purchases**: The number of sales that happened because of the ad.
- **Website Purchase Conversion Value**: The total amount earned from the purchases due to your ad.
- **Frequency**: The number of times each person you have reached sees the ad on average. There can be times when you see a dip in your ad performance, and that could be because Facebook is showing the ad to the same set of people several times.
- **Reach**: The number of unique people you managed to reach through your ad.
- **Relevance Score**: Based on the first 500 impressions, it measures how relevant the ad is to the people who are being targeted. This impacts your budget significantly.

- **Budget**: The amount you can afford to spend on your ad set – daily or in total.
- **Cost per Result**: The amount it takes to achieve the ad objective set by you.
- **CPM**: The amount you pay for 1000 impressions.

Even after selecting the criteria from this list, you can break down these further to analyze the performance of your ads depending on various factors. For example, devices that were used to make the purchase, impact of gender on the performance of the ad, and so on. A great, effective practice that you can use is having useful naming conventions at each level of your Ads Manager. By doing this, you will be able to view who you are targeting and what you are testing.

Mistake 8: Audience and the Offer Mismatch

When you try to build a new audience on Facebook, it tends to add complexity to the ad creation process. This is mainly because when you are building a new audience, you are actually trying to nurture existing people and generate new awareness to convert some of them. All this creates complications in the process. Things become more complicated when the two most important ingredients go wrong – the target audience and the used offer. To see the difference, you can run the ad in two different scenarios:

- Targeting the right set of audience
- Poorly targeted

When you look at the results generated by the ad in these two different scenarios, you will see a huge difference in the number of clicks achieved for a CPC under these two scenarios. So, it can be said that –

Ad success = the right audience + the right offer

You can then determine the right temperature of each ad and the stage they are at in the sales funnel.

Top-of-the-Funnel – This portion of the sales funnel comprises of all those who do not know about your brand. Therefore, you cannot just show them the Buy Now ad because this audience hardly knows you and would not be interested in what you are offering. Instead of asking them to buy your product straight away, do things so that they know about your brand. You can generate interest by showing them content related to your brand in the form of articles, blogs, videos, images and so on.

Middle of the Funnel – This portion of the sales funnel comprises of all the people who have interacted with you or visited your website. They know about your brand and what you talk about. This doesn't mean that they know what you do, or they might know what you do but might not be convinced that you are capable of doing it the right way. For this set of people, you can create low-ticket items like free consultations, demos, webinars and so on.

Bottom of the Funnel – This part of the sales funnel comprises of all those who have bought things from you in the past or shown interest in your offering based on a promotion or consultation. These are the people who are ready to buy and hence you can show them the 'Buy Now' ads to promote your offering.

Mistake 9: Over-relying on the ad targeting

Custom audiences are the ones who convert the most for the least amount you spend on the ads. It is just like retargeting because you know what the person wants and when he wants it based on his previous behavior (such as adding something to their cart). This is the reason why the average click-through-rate of retargeting ads is ten times more than the regular ads. The problem is you cannot use the Custom Audiences located at the top of sales funnel when you are trying to build a new audience. To find these people, you will have to use interest-based targeting and select attributes like their industry, jobs, or Facebook pages they follow. However, there is a lot more to it than just these attributes. Therefore, it is always good to build a Custom Audience quickly when you are trying to reach new people. You can create the custom set using content type, such as 'people who viewed at least 3 seconds of your video', 'people who viewed at least 10 seconds of your video' and so on. This can get you lot of views in a few minutes, but at some point, you will be forced to use interest-based targeting. To handle this, you can further refine this audience using 'interest-intersection and exclusions'.

To do this:

Select any of the given interests and you will be able to get large audiences that like these two interests. when you click on the tab 'any of these', you will get only a small section of the audience who like both. In addition to this, you can also select interests that you wish to exclude from this list. Select what you want to exclude, and then click 'None of these'. This way using interest-intersection and exclusions, you can see what works for you and what does not.

Chapter 14:

Facebook Social Plugins, Facebook Badges, and Facebook Notes

Social plugins on Facebook are an easy way to build a website that is Facebook integrated with little effort on your part. You do not have to be a web developer to build these plugins; all you have to do it copy and paste the little pieces into any document on Facebook. If you have these social plugins handy, you can reach out to a greater audience. This way you are giving them more options to engage with you.

Considering this fact, Facebook offers advertisers a lot of options to integrate their platforms with the websites. It makes sense for the website owners or the advertisers to take advantage of the power of Facebook on their site. Facebook is the most used identity considering the number of people who sign up for this site. The best part is that these social plugins can be implemented on any website with no coding knowledge required by the user. You need to know some of these plugins and the reason behind having them integrated onto your site.

LIKE: This is probably the most used and best recognized social plugin of Facebook. It can be placed on any page of your website and can be set in a way that it is targeted to Like the page the button is placed on. For instance, if you have four pages in your site, and you place a Like button on each of these four pages, then it will create a Like to your Home page each time these are clicked. So, if you want to add a Like button to your page, just visit the developer's page and then enter the URL you wish visitors to Like. You can later customize other features, such as the layout of the page, show who all liked it, number of people who liked it, the color of the button and so on. Now you have the Like button incorporated into your website page. If you are wondering how is it going to help you, the Like is a brilliant social proof that shows people visiting your page how many others have liked it before them. Also, when a user likes a page, it shows up in his feed and hence all his friends get to know about his 'Like'. This way you can engage users and their friends and increase the social support count for your website.

ACTIVITY FEED: The Activity Feed is a place where all the recent activities of a user on the website are shown. It has all the activities on the website by friends of a user and also the number of times certain content was recommended. This helps others know what their friends like, follow, and share. To add an Activity Feed plugin onto your website, visit the documentation page and enter the domain of your website. You can then customize other attributes, such as colors, header, font, and size of the activity feed box. If you want to 'Show Recommendations', place the code on your website.

RECOMMENDATIONS: This is quite similar to the Activity Feed. It shows the number of times the content is Liked by the users and the recent top content of the users. It doesn't matter if the user is logged into Facebook or not. If he is, he will see any friends who have Liked any of the content on his page. This will help you determine the top content on your website and you can then use it to find new visitors. To include the Recommendations button on your website, visit the documentation page and enter the domain of your website. You can then customize other features, such as colors, font, and so on.

COMMENTS: This plugin allows you to include the Facebook Comments feature on any of the pages of your website. It can be a great way of making a static page interactive by incorporating comments on the feedback of the users. Some users use the comment plugin to include their website link to the page on which they are commenting. This way they can expose their link to a friend of the Facebook user through their News Feed. There is one additional step involved in adding the Comments plugin than just adding and getting the code onto the documentation page. This requires to first register your website as an application with Facebook by creating the application. Enter the name of your company or website as the App Name and then Agree to the terms and conditions of Facebook. You will be shown a captcha, after which you can enter other details about the website or application. The most important thing is the privacy policy URL and the Terms of Service URL. Enter the website URL and domain correctly so that Facebook authenticates on the right domain.

LOGIN: Users can use this button to connect with you using their Facebook login. This plugin can be used to show the number of people who are connected to your website or collect information using more complex aspects of the site.

Facebook Badges for your Business

Badges are small, but dynamic in their functioning! They are the versatile Facebook Badges, the updating widgets that you may utilize to display contents of your Facebook pages outside the social networking website. Of course, this does not mean that anybody and everybody can step into your private online 'home' without permission! It just means that you may drop the badges onto any publishing platform or website of your choice, and your choice alone, to perform various functions! For instance, you may display your Facebook photographs on your personal web pages in the form of a slideshow. Then again, you may allow people to view your Facebook profile directly via a link placed on a blog or your business website. Use these tools to promote your Facebook Page or place a snippet of your Facebook profile in your online curriculum vitae. Facebook Badges will aid you in sharing relevant information with relevant people! In turn, your business will be able to progress in the right direction.

Creating Different Badges

Facebook offers four different types of badges:

Profile Badge

This is marvelous for sharing relevant information from your Facebook Page with other trustworthy websites. To begin with, you have to log in to your Facebook account and move to the landing page connected with Facebook Badges. The kind of badge that you need to create is a profile badge. Therefore, opt for the Profile badge option from the choices given. Then, it is time to select the layout for this badge, or in other words, adjust the settings to your liking. The layout may be horizontal, column-like in nature, or vertical. Decide which one is most suitable for your 'business' purpose. It also depends upon the kind of page size, which is available on the user website to attach the badge. Click on the Edit button on the page and select your layout.

Now you can customize your profile page. Among the various options displayed on the menu, choose whatever you do not mind being made public. For example, this could include the profile picture you wish to display, your professional name, hometown, current city, birthday, email address, mobile number, your networks, etc. As soon as you complete your selections, press the 'Save' button. This action indicates to the system that the Facebook user has created a profile badge, and in turn, it has to generate a code. This is a snippet of HTML code. Paste this code wherever you would like it to appear, such as onto a Blogger/Typepad website. However, ensure that you select the appropriate icon on this site for the automatic creation of a sidebar widget. Alternatively, you may place this code in the footer of your personal page whenever the pop-up screen shows up. If you use Google Plus, you may wish to create a Google+ profile widget.

When you fill in the code at various places, it focuses first on sorting out the most recent contents on your Facebook Page. Second, it provides links that act as connections between other websites and this social networking website.

Photo Badge

Similar to the option for a profile badge, there is an option for the photo badge. Select it, if you desire to create this kind of a badge to share your Facebook photographs with visitors entering your official business website or your personal blog.

At the outset, decide if you want a two-column, horizontal, or vertical layout. Additionally, figure out how many pictures can be and should be displayed on your photo badge. Note that if you want a large number of photographs on view, you will need to enhance the size of the badge. You will be able to make a final decision by looking at the preview of your photo badge. You should be able to see it on the right-hand-side of the Facebook Page. When you are ready with your preferences and settings, click on the 'Save' button. You will be given access to a code. Paste this code on the website that you have chosen for your profile badge. You will not have to update this code every time you upload new pictures on your Facebook Page. The updating will happen on its own, due to the links that the profile badge has provided earlier.

Page Badge

This is another option on the menu of Facebook Badges. Follow the same steps that you did for creating the other two badges. Decide what kind of orientation you want for your badge and examine the preview on the right-hand-side of the Facebook Page. Only you, as the legal administrator of this particular Facebook account, can utilize this feature to promote your business on this social networking website.

Like Badge

Choose the Like Badge option when you want to share information with others about all your favorite web pages on the World Web. If they agree with your selections, they will Like them too.

To begin with, find a page on the Internet that has information that you like and would like to display on your badge. Next, post this content on your website. Then, opt for a Fan Page so that you can obtain a code. Place this code on your website. You will be able to review the preview of this badge on the right-hand-side of your Facebook Page.

Verifying the Facebook Business Page

If you are a business, it is imperative that you present yourself as reliable and trustworthy. This becomes more difficult online than offline since people are not able to come face-to-face with you. Furthermore, your regular customers, or even would-be consumers, may be far away in some other part of the world. Therefore, when you plan to use the Facebook platform for promoting/advertising your business, you need to seek its approval. This social networking site offers a checkmark as a stamp of approval. When visitors see the mark, they gain assurance about your authenticity. Even though the page is official in nature, the very fact that Facebook confirms that you are exactly who you say you are and will build trust in any and every visitor.

Another reason is that verification builds credibility. The first impression is the lasting impression! The adage stretches to online business platforms too! In fact, it is even more important to create an eye-catching impression within a few seconds in the virtual world. This is because people have short attention spans, especially when browsing websites on the Internet. Therefore, if a visitor to your Business Page on your Facebook account notices the check mark of dependability immediately, then you have won half the battle already!

A third reason is that the verification badge helps to remove confusion. For example, it could be that your particular business spreads across several pages. Would-be customers and regular fans are going to become extremely confused about your precise location when they view so many web pages. However, when they view the verification symbol on your Facebook Page, they will immediately comprehend that this is the official platform of your business.

The fourth reason relates to visibility in search engines. Admittedly, like every other businessperson, you would like to have your platform showing up in the higher rankings. Once you complete the verification process on Facebook, you will witness a pop-up. This pop-up carries the message that your verified page will show up in an enhanced position in search engine results, thanks to possessing a verified badge. This is similar to the SEO you witness on Google.com.

Please note: not everyone, who has an account on Facebook is eligible for verification. Otherwise, Facebook would have a tough time with the millions and millions, who are its members! You have to be a government official, a reasonably well-known business and brand, a celebrity/public figure linked to politics, entertainment, sports or the media. If you are just a start-up company or a small, local business, you may not find it so easy to gain a Blue or Gray badge from Facebook.

As for everything else, you are required to submit certain official documents if you want a verification of your Facebook Page. These include passport, genuine birth certificate (signed by an authentic official), driver's license, and incorporation articles (if you belong to or endorse the media, entertainment establishments, or sports companies).

Type of Badge

Facebook uses a special method to inform visitors who peruse diverse accounts and pages on this social networking site that what they are seeing is authentic. It supplies a Verified Badge to the owner of the account especially if he/she is engaged in using the website for promoting a business. This badge may be a blue or a gray circle. A tic mark accompanies each circle.

If you need to confirm that a site is indeed a media company/personality, a public figure, a renowned brand, or a large business, you might choose the Blue Badge verification process. At the same time, not all brands, public figures, and celebrities opt for displaying Blue Badges. They do not need them because they do not have an online/offline business!

A Gray Badge: Anyone with a small business chooses this particular mode of verification. You could be a start-up venture or own a brick-and-mortar shop. The social networking site confirms your authenticity via the Gray Badge. If you have multiple branches of the same shop, you will need to verify every Facebook Page for every shop via a Gray Badge. Unlike the Blue Badge that generally caters to people, entertainment, media, governmental agencies, and sports, the Gray Badge favors local businesses, companies, and organizations. You do not have the option of 'purchasing' a Blue or Gray Badge. Only Facebook authorities can bestow a badge on you.

Verify your Profile or Personal Page with a Blue Badge

Facebook exhibits a higher preference for two categories: Profile and Personal. Therefore, if your application automatically falls into either of them, you are lucky! Your verification process will move forward much faster. If your personal page does not meet the required specifications, you may go to the "About" column and change it to 'public figure'. Alternatively, you may convert your personal page into a profile, as well as convert all your friends on that page into 'Likes'.

While you are getting your Facebook Page ready for activation, you will witness diverse information boxes showing up in the 'About' section. They are in alignment with your page's category and demand that you fill in basic information. These basic details must include accurate information about who you are and what you are (biography, official website, phone number, address, awards received, and so on). Do not skimp on the details. Supply as much relevant information as you can without actually focusing too much on the personal.

If you are keen to get a Facebook profile verified, ensure that you provide authentic information about yourself and include a website address that you have registered in your name in the "About" section. If you want your business to grow, you cannot afford to keep your profile private. You will have to make it public, not by choice, but by default. Only then will visitors and regular customers be able to keep track of you and follow you. Most importantly, do not rush to obtain a Blue Badge immediately after creating a public profile. Wait until you have at least a healthy number of followers. Around 500 or so should suffice in the initial stages. The numbers will serve to convince Facebook about the genuineness of your request.

Facebook used to provide a form link to submit a request for verification. Therefore, you will have to try another method which may or may not work. There is no harm in trying. To begin with, look for a blue question mark on the top right-hand corner of the Facebook Page or it might be on the Home page. When a few options show up, choose Report a Problem. Follow this up with Something Is Not Working. When the system responds with a query, 'Where is the Problem', opt for Pages.

Use the text box to write an introduction of yourself and provide a couple of reasons for requesting the verification. These reasons must be compelling enough to prompt Facebook authorities to take action. You will have to decide for yourself what to write since only you are acquainted with the product or service that you are offering. Furthermore, every businessperson has his/her own reasons for wanting to advertise on Facebook via these badges. Do not forget to place the URL of your official website in this box. Place links to informative press articles or a page on Wikipedia too. Do not write lengthy and boring content; make sure your content is to the point and easy to comprehend.

After you have finished, move to the Upload Screenshots section. You need a valid ID issued by your country's government and upload it here. You are done! All you can do is to wait for a reply from Facebook.

Verify your Business Page with a Gray Badge

A Gray Badge is much easier to obtain than a Blue Badge. Facebook favors awarding more Gray Badges rather than

Blue Badges. If your page falls into the category of company, local business, or organization, then it is definitely eligible to receive a Gray Badge. If you are an administrator, your page displays a cover photo and a profile picture and is eligible for verification. You can find such an option in the settings on your page itself.

Since you desire to own a Gray Badge, provide a business document, such as a recent telephone bill in your name to the verifiers. Alternatively, you may give the public telephone number that you use during business hours. It is imperative that this number is a public listing and not a private one.

The procedure you must follow to obtain verification:

Find the option called Settings on the top of your Facebook Page, and click on it. Select 'General' from the choices that are shown. Next, move to Page Verification. Opt for 'Verify this Page' and click on Get Started. Now fill in the relevant information that proves that you are serious about advertising your business on this social networking site. Enter the name of the country where you have the headquarters of your business correctly. Decide on the language of communication with your visitors/customers. Do not forget to enter your 'business' phone number. When you are through, press the button 'Call Me Now'. Facebook will call you and provide you with a verification code. As soon you receive this code, enter it in the space provided, and press Continue. The code is a four-digit number. As soon as you click on Continue, you will receive certain instructions to follow along with diverse options.

How Does Facebook Respond to Verification Requests

You may still be wondering if it is truly beneficial to possess a Blue or Gray Badge. Yes, it is beneficial because the badge will lend credibility to your business account. After all, you cannot blame people for fearing scammers, fraudsters, or imposters. There are plenty of them in the virtual world! Your existing clients, as well as would-be clients, will appreciate your intelligence in using social media wisely. Above all, your ego will receive a huge boost when your verified pages are displayed as highly ranked pages on search engines and Facebook's Graph Search.

Facebook will get back to you within 48 hours or week, to inform you that you are eligible for verification in the form of a Gray Badge! With regard to a Blue Badge, however, the waiting period cannot be determined. Facebook may reach a decision within just three days, or it may take 45 days. As soon as you submit an application for verification, whether it is for a Blue or Gray Badge, keep regular track of messages in your support inbox. Sometimes, Facebook authorities reject verification requests. It could be because of any of the following reasons. For instance, maybe you did not provide reasons that were compelling enough to acquire a Blue or Gray badge. You may not have provided an appropriate official ID. The ID could be so blurry that Facebook did not feel it was genuine. Perhaps you had insufficient native content on your Facebook Page. Facebook refuses to indulge 'dead' pages. The social networking site may feel that you are not popular enough yet to merit verification. Facebook expects you to feature on Forbes and similar websites sometime. It follows that if you do not have a high-quality press, Wikipedia or Wiki will not feature your business or you on its pages.

Facebook Notes

Facebook Notes have been around for quite some time now, and are as useful today as they were when this social networking site first launched them. The idea is to allow members to express their opinions and feelings through short or lengthy content so that friends and fans may read them. The same would look rather odd when placed in the 'status update' box!

Interesting Features

Here are the options for Facebook Note.

- Choose a style - italics, bold, code, underline, or quotes.
- Different sections/large quote areas in your content and provide headings for each section.
- A header/cover image to every Note, measuring 1200 x 445 pixels.
- If you have unique links and hyperlinks to share, include them in the Note.
- Present matter in the form of numbered/bulleted lists.
- Add photos.
- Crop and resize photographs to fit them into appropriate spaces. The maximum height permissible is 720 pixels.
- A caption for each image/photograph to make it even more memorable.

- You cannot embed videos into your Facebook Notes, but you can definitely embed your FB Notes onto your personal blog.
- Tag your favorite people, groups, or pages in the text.
- View your Notes in your profile. These Notes possess their own 'feed' area, and are, therefore, far more accessible than 'posts'.
- Save the draft of a particular Note in order to spend more time to polish it later.
- Comment upon something, express a 'Like', or share something. This will help in increasing your engagement with friends, would-be customers, and regular visitors.
- Maintain privacy by allowing specific individuals or groups to view your FB Notes. However, they are bound to show up in Google searches.

Create a Facebook Note

If you have stepped into www.facebook.com/notes, you are in the General Notes region. You will know by seeing the Notes News Feed. The option available is, "Write a Note". On the other hand, if you have reached your personal profile, you will be able to click on the "Add Note" icon and begin. Although each platform works equally well, your profile page is a better option for promoting your business venture.

To Enable Facebook Notes:

Log in to your Facebook Page.

On your profile page, you should be able to view an option titled "More". The header photograph is directly below it in the horizontal menu.

When you click on it, you will see Manage Sections in the drop-down menu.

Click on Notes as confirmation.

Whenever you opt for "More," you will see the Notes option pop up.

Clicking on it will allow you to create and manage new Facebook Notes, via the + Add Note feature where you will display the contents of the Note.

If you were a business person, you would obviously like to make your Facebook Notes easily accessible to your fans. Therefore, you could go to the Timeline on your Facebook Page and opt for the "More" tab. The next option is Manage Tabs, followed by Add or Remove Tabs. Choose the Add the Notes app. Later on, you will have to re-arrange all the tabs on your Facebook Page because Notes are considered more important than the other things on display. To begin writing a new Note, move to the Share menu at the top of your Timeline. There is a Q&A, Event+ icon in it. When you click on it, you will view a drop-down menu, and select 'Note'.

Write the Contents

Every Note must have a compelling/catchy title to arouse curiosity in your visitors/customers/fans. Your contents may relate to your own thoughts. They may even relate to something interesting that you feel like sharing from another source. If you are copying and pasting something from another source, please give due credit to the author/website, even in the Note. If you are a regular blog writer on your business website, you may use the Facebook Note to drive traffic. Present a summary of your expert contents (latest blog post) on the Note. Do not forget to add a link to the complete article on the Note!

You may create a Facebook Note comprised of supplementary content. Create a link to your original blog post and the Facebook Note, or link the Note to your article. A Facebook Note can play the role of an influential communicator to keep existing customers on board, as well as attracting potential consumers to visit your establishment. You can use the Facebook Note in the form of a biography, or about your business (product/service). Alternatively, you may introduce a new service/product, and provide a link, which will take the visitor to the landing page of your official website or where the product/service is on display. Facebook Notes offer a great platform to keep your existing fans/followers/customers updated about your business or a similar industry. If there are promotions or contests on Facebook, share the details with people. After all, you are the sponsor! To express your appreciation for your fans/customers, use Facebook Notes to recognize them, specifically if they are in the top rankings!

Format Facebook Notes

In the main content area, you should be able to see some icons on the left-hand side. There are diverse formatting options contained in a list. Your text may be simple and plain, bulleted, quoted, numbered, or have headings. If you highlight any part of the writing in the box, you should see a small menu pop up. This is for putting emphasis on specific words/phrases via mono, bold, underlining or italics. Use the "@" symbol in front of their names, in order to connect to other individuals and their pages. If you use hyperlinks, you will be able to connect to a broader audience. The quotation mark icon placed to the left of your Facebook Note will help you draw attention toward a specific quote/paragraph. Do not stop experimenting with diverse formats until you discover what suits your Facebook profile and your target audience the best!

Make Every Note Visually Appealing

Everybody loves to view photographs, especially if they have captions attached to them. Therefore, make your cover/header photograph eye-catching. If you have great images on your Facebook Page itself, choose one of them. Alternatively, upload something new. You may get help from the photo icon that is next to the list icon. Your followers will notice the pictures as they scroll through News Feed. You are aware of the dimensions of a cover/header photograph, so keep that in mind as you aim for the best resolution. Do not try to enlarge small/tiny photographs in order to fit into the space provided. They may appear blurry or grainy as they are made larger. Try to use images that are as close to 1200 x 445 pixels as possible. You may include as many pictures as you want in your Facebook Note, but make sure that they are clear, reasonably sized, and captioned. The idea of writing a Facebook Note is to initiate a discussion with your fans/followers. It is also a platform for sourcing ideas for future Notes. Make it attention-grabbing!

Publish your Notes

You can save a lengthy Note as a draft and polish it later on prior to publishing. You will find the Save option at the bottom of the editor. You can publish a Facebook Note only manually. It is not an automated process. Facebook discontinued this in 2011.

Whenever you publish a Facebook Note, it is imperative that you make it 'visible' in the right way. The options for privacy are located in the drop-down menu available near the Save/Publish icons. You can choose to make your contents public, offer it to your friends to view and read, keep it just for yourself, or choose a custom option. If you have kept it open for friends or the public, your Note will appear in all their News Feeds. Some may just 'Like' it. Some may want to comment on what you have written.

Supervise your Notes

If you have enabled "More" on your Facebook profile page, you will always have access to old and new Notes. You may want to make some changes in your existing Notes at times. First, move your cursor to the title of a Note. Click to open it. Look at the right-hand-corner and you will see an Edit icon. Use it for making the necessary changes. You may want to delete some areas of the text or update existing content. You may want to modify the privacy settings for this particular Note. If you want to delete the Note completely, use the Delete icon at the bottom of your page.

Sometimes, your friends/followers publish Facebook Notes and they tag you. If you wish to view these Notes, go to the Notes about (your name) tab.

Read Notes Displayed by Other Users

You have a News Feed on your Facebook Page too. When your friends/followers create New Notes, you will be able to see them on this Feed. However, they tend to be lost at times among other types of information. Therefore, you can visit www.facebook.com/notes instead, where the filtered News Feed version displays only Facebook Notes. An alternative is to reach out to your friends' profiles directly and look for posts in the Notes section. After all, their profile pages are similar to yours! If a particular friend has put up a collection of Facebook Notes only for a close circle of friends, select "More," and then, Notes on this person's profile page.

Facebook Notes are Important

You may wonder why you need to create Facebook Notes when there is plenty of space to post everything on the Facebook Page itself. If you have your official blog for marketing your business, you begin to wonder even more! Regardless, it still makes sense to create Facebook Notes for advertising your product or service. There are several reasons for this. Facebook is a social networking site and has a wider reach than your personal/official blog as it has over a million users. Imagine leveraging the power of this vast audience to drive traffic to your official website, via clicks on links in your text! The News Feed will help project Facebook Notes and even Google will be able to index your Notes. You may strive to run FB advertisements in order to target an FB Note. Facebook Notes are not only pleasing to the eye but also very easy to create.

Using Facebook Notes to Market your Business

Facebook Notes as 'advertisements' can be used for your business in several ways.

Become a Blogger

Like everyone else, you may have been wishing to pen your thoughts on paper, or rather on the Internet. You may not have had the time to set up a blogging site, or even write! With the advent of the Internet, blogging has become an integral part of every business in the virtual and the real world.

You may find it slightly difficult in the beginning. However, as you continue to write consistently, you will gain confidence. Spend some time to explore every topic under the sun, which will ultimately focus on the product/service that your business has to offer. Even the comments that follow every blog that you post on the Facebook Note will give you new ideas for newer articles. Although you are on a 'rented' platform currently, you may soon move to a self-owned one as the situation improves. You should strive to take your marketing strategy to a completely new level and wonderful results will follow!

Write a Summary

You may have written some blogs earlier, not for your own website. If they are relevant to your business, your fans/followers/customers should know about them. Therefore, write a short summary of each blog on a Facebook Note, and publish it. At the bottom of each summary, include a link that will take the reader directly to the full article.

Embed FB Notes in Other Blog Posts

When you have selected the published Facebook Note that you wish to use, click on it. When the drop-down menu appears, note the code that you will require for your official blog. This is assuming that you already have your own blogging website. Create content around the Facebook Note that you have borrowed from your Facebook Page. Keep the blog's contents informative. The Facebook Note encourages engagement (Like, Share, or Comment) from the readers.

Reach out to Fellow Bloggers

You can include hyperlinks in your Note. You can tag people on other Facebook pages via @ and their respective names. Whenever you tag somebody, inform that individual about it through email, on Facebook itself, via Facebook Messenger, or on Twitter.

At the same time, remember that you are not doing this for fun. You have serious promotional strategies for your business. Therefore, connect with prominent bloggers who will prove useful to you in the business arena.

Share Notes with Friends

When your fans/followers read the contents, they may wish to share them on their own Facebook profiles, Facebook pages, or Facebook Groups. In turn, their friends get to see your FB Notes too! Thus, you manage to reach a large audience comprising of both known and unknown people.

If you include hyperlinks to other websites that have shown your articles on their pages, related content on your own official website, or products/services, visitors may acquire greater knowledge about what you do and even enhance your sales.

Promote your Business

Decide on the product/service that you sell. You could use the services of Shortstack to prepare a Facebook Landing page tab for your items. Alternatively, you may prefer to use your own creativity and launch your product/products, or service/services, through a Facebook Note. Add relevant photographs to substantiate the descriptions. Hyperlinks lead readers to pages displaying each service/product separately. This makes it easy for people to purchase from you.

Pin to Top

There's a 'Pin to Top' feature on your Facebook Page. It is a great tool for improving the visibility of your Facebook Notes. Every Note will show up at the top of your Facebook Page. Of course, you may pin only one Note at a time. Therefore, keep replacing old Notes with new ones regularly.

Instruct Would-be Students

Sometimes, several customers request answers to the same questions repeatedly. In fact, they often relate to actions that they must take with regard to your business. What you could do is answer each question on a separate Facebook Note and publish it. As you archive each question and answer, you obtain a storehouse of data. They may become the FAQs on your official website.

Every Note receives its own URL, and if you want to share it, perform a right-click with your mouse on your selected date. Then opt for Copy Link Address.

Create Facebook Advertisements

Use your creativity to create a new Facebook advertisement to help you promote your published Facebook Note. Prepare the advertisement in such a way that it targets the common interests of your readers, as well as other Facebook pages that they Liked.

Write a Weekly Summary

Perhaps you have written five or six posts about a certain topic throughout the week. These posts should be on your official blog. Prepare a summary of all the articles. The summary that shows up on your Facebook Note should include the title of the first article, a couple of sentences about the content and a link to it. Similarly, provide the title of the second article, brief contents, and link. Thus, your fans/followers will be able to gauge your expertise through your summary and links to full articles.

Conclusion

Thanks for downloading *"Facebook Advertising: The Guide to Dominating the Largest Social Media Platform"*.

I hope this guide helped you understand the basics as well as advanced features of Facebook Advertising. It will help you create and advertise Facebook pages, events, groups and so on. I hope it helped you gain insights into how to promote your brand or product on Facebook, which is the most powerful social media platform today.

Anyone can register and create an account or Fan Page for a corporate or personal identity and practice social media branding. The trick is in doing the job effectively and in achieving the right outcomes. Here is a quick snapshot of some tips on branding effectively on Facebook.

Post consistently and regularly: This is undoubtedly the first and the most significant step to good branding. Do not be irregular in posting or take indefinite breaks as this will only divert your viewers and they will lose interest in your brand. Instead, plan a schedule or make an editorial calendar that will help you plan and execute your updates in an organized manner.

Interact with your audience: It is extremely important to interact and respond to your viewers' Likes and Comments. This will create the belief and conviction that you care about your audience and they will also build interest and trust in your brand. This will help you create effective and unique branding.

Choose visuals: Having endless texts and messages will not really attract a large crowd. As a picture speaks a thousand words, choose more visuals and fewer texts. This will help convey your message more efficiently.

Have some fun: All work and no play is surely a turn-off. Make an attempt to plan exciting contests, giveaways, games, and events to keep your audience interested. The more the merrier. This will also give rise to creativity and help in achieving higher goals and corresponding outcomes.

Strike a balance: There is a clear demarcation between being adequate and going overboard. Do not flood your viewer's newsfeed with endless updates as this will really put them off and could force them to Unlike your page. Instead, strike a balance and post when needed and smartly start on the right foot with your audience.

Focus on events and discounts: If your company is having a special event or some great offer, make sure to specify it and brief your viewers. This will help to keep them updated on what's going on and also help in making your brand more popular and successful.

Cater to your audience: Categorize your audience and divide them into groups. Form content that is likely to interest the groups and post accordingly. Maintain a balance and post information that will complement your business but also match your customer's interests and preferences. Initially, it will be difficult to decipher the varied interests, so keep experimenting. Post all kinds of updates and then do a study as to which post has achieved the highest number of Likes, Comments, and Shares and plan accordingly. Encourage your audience to share your posts and to spread the word. This way you can expand your social media network and reach out to an even higher number of people.

Capture it in motion: Try to include a video once in a while. Incorporate storytelling methods to pass on your message in an innovative way. This is a great way to keep your audience interested.

Now, aren't you eager to start your first advertising campaign on Facebook? Get started right away!

Made in the USA
Lexington, KY
04 December 2018